D0917617

The My...

The Myth of "Fit"

Unlock New Leader Success with High-Impact Onboarding

LINDA S. REESE, PhD

WITH

STEPHANIE HENDERSON

Ventura Pines
Publishing

Copyright © 2017 Linda Reese
All rights reserved.

No part of this publication may be reproduced, stored in a retrieval system, or transmitted, in any form or by any means—electronic, mechanical, photocopying, recording, scanning, or otherwise—without prior written permission. Requests to the publisher for permission should be addressed to: Ventura Pines Publishing, PO Box 334, Blacklick, OH 43004, or sent to info@venturapinespublishing.com.

This book contains a number of case studies and anecdotes to demonstrate the significance of subject matter in the chapters they are located. These stories and examples are composites of numerous experiences and occurrences that we have encountered. The characters are not intended to represent, identify, or denote any particular individual. Therefore, any names, characters, businesses, places, events, and incidents are used in a fictitious manner. Any resemblance to actual persons, living or dead, or events is purely coincidental.

Readers should take into consideration that website addresses or online publications offered as citations or sources for further information may have been changed or removed between the time this publication was written and when it was read.

ISBN-13: 978-0-9985023-4-2
Library of Congress Control Number: 2017905576
Published by Ventura Pines Publishing
Printed by CreateSpace

Includes notes and index.

Cover image: @rawpixel/123RF.com
Cover image manipulation and design: Jennifer Belvel
Author photography: Alan Geho www.ralphoto.com

Contents

This book is dedicated to Diane Downey, a thought leader and valued mentor; and all the New Leaders who allow us to share their journey.

Introduction

Why another book on leader onboarding—aren't there enough? We all know about the importance of getting it right from the start, building 90-day plans and making quick hits. And most big companies already do onboarding—so another book won't shed new light, right?

We beg to differ. In nearly 20 years of supporting leader transitions, we have learned at least a couple of important things: Leaders who should be successful often aren't, and employers attribute failure to them being a poor "fit." We believe, with few exceptions, that New Leaders really derail because they haven't been set up for success. And that it's the joint responsibility of the New Leader and the company. Thus our title: *The Myth of "Fit."* Onboarding into a new leadership role is fraught with risk, but that risk is often overlooked.

This takes us to the rationale for this book—that successful onboarding isn't about orientation or "low-hanging fruit," but instead about recognizing and mitigating New Leader risk. Or it should be. You may find this book non-linear, because rather than sequentially laying out an ideal onboarding path, we focus on the (often hidden) risk factors associated with New Leader transition. You will find illustrated examples of when and why New Leaders struggle. And also risk management techniques and tools—your keys to proactively unlocking New Leader success.

Foreword

As an organization designer, I frequently have the opportunity to observe executives as they reshape their direct-report teams. New hires are brought in, internals are elevated, or existing players given new roles. These leadership changes are intended to create the right power dynamics, talent profiles, and conversations that will support new organization models and drive better business outcomes.

But sometimes, even with a solid strategy, structured organizational design, and sound talent-assessment work, new leaders falter or even fail. The root cause is that the organization does not set them up for success, especially during the critical first few months. In a typical scenario, the high-profile external hire—originally brought in with great fanfare and promise—leaves after 18 months, frustrated.

I look forward to giving my clients, who are business executives and HR leaders, this book. With *The Myth of "Fit": Unlock New Leader Success with High-Impact Onboarding*, Linda Reese and Stephanie Henderson have created a practical guide for ensuring that the hiring manager, the newly-placed leader, and the organization are all prepared and able to navigate what can be a complex transition—even under the best of circumstances.

The authors take a "design" approach to the challenge of new leader fit. Rather than focusing solely on personality, fit, and behavior, they also consider ways the organization can work with the new leader to architect the system, and build their onboarding program for key hires. This includes thoughtfully crafting and articulating roles (so accountabilities and authority become clear) and setting organizational structure, processes, and resources in place to support success.

The paradoxes new leaders face are very real. This book provides tremendous value in simply unveiling these paradoxes, and recognizing that the organizational and personal dynamics of leadership change are complex. For successful assimilation, both the new leader and the organization must adapt. Choreographing this dance is not easy. For example, all new leaders grapple with the dilemma of whether to be patient and assess the finer details of their situation, or take immediate action and make changes to demonstrate their impact. Of course, if someone is placed in a role to turn around a situation, action will be expected. However, many leadership transitions occur as the result of normal succession. Too often we see these new leaders rush to restructure their teams, resulting in unnecessary churn. In an attempt to demonstrate value, they undermine their credibility and destabilize the organization. The authors provide useful perspective and guidance on this and other common paradoxes.

This book has special meaning for me. It builds on the insights of the late Diane Downey, who was a mentor, colleague, and friend for over 15 years. Diane introduced me to organization design and talent management. She was a true systems thinker, who encouraged organizations to share the accountability for new leader onboarding in her seminal work, *Assimilating New Leaders*. With *The Myth of "Fit"* Linda Reese and Stephanie Henderson combine their own research, business experience, and the wisdom of others to make a significant and innovative contribution to the field.

Amy Kates
Managing Partner, Kates Kesler Organization Consulting
New York
December 2016

The Myth of "Fit"

I

The Myth of "Fit"
Unlock New Leader Success with High-Impact Onboarding

Gretchen's Story

I accepted a newly-created position as a Vice President for product launches, with responsibility for Asia Pacific and Latin America, at a fast-growing beauty brand. In a highly competitive environment, with the organization scrambling to keep up, my boss Greg told me I would have to drive results for the regions.

My first assignment was to carry out two key product launches. Everything was going well until I encountered a major setback with resources. During the selection process, the company talked about my team as though they were solid-line reporting relationships, but I soon discovered they were only dotted-line associates from R&D, Marketing, and Planning.

Given my accountabilities, it would be difficult to meet expected results with no direct reports. Adding to that, I found myself managing a large operation with a business model that I had to adapt to both Asia Pacific and Latin America regions (vastly different markets). I was concerned

1

about the fragmentation of my role, but proceeded onward.

Feeling pressure to deliver quickly, I assembled an ad-hoc team. With everyone spread across two continents and 12 time zones, I traveled to meet each team member face-to-face. Since I had placed a significant focus on relationships early in the transition, my feedback scores (delivered through *LevelSet: Early Feedback*) were high enough to be typical of New Leaders who will experience long-term success.

Then, four or five months into my role, the Vice President of HR started hearing concerns that I wasn't generating expected results. My boss Greg approached me and said, "Frankly, I'm not sure if you do have the skills for this job."

That was only the beginning of my struggles. Within a short time, I saw my reputation tarnished. I learned I was being labeled a "poor fit"—no matter how hard I worked.

At this point, I feared my employment was coming to a swift and dramatic end. The company seemed ready to cut its losses, and start recruiting the "perfect" replacement. But in my defense, I felt I had entered the job with others holding unreasonable expectations—given the lack of resources and failure to properly support meeting demanding goals. The organization was holding me to a standard <u>no one</u> could live up to. So, I decided to take action, and arranged a meeting with my boss and Janet, the head of HR, to see what we could do.

As we talked through the details of the first months in the role, Janet challenged Greg to look at things from my perspective. She said, "Greg, let's review the hard facts. The organization never set this role up for success, and a global product launch without dedicated resources was doomed no matter who led the charge. So instead of blaming or replacing Gretchen, I think we should try to identify and remove significant stumbling blocks, so that she can meet her goals."

After that meeting, Greg restructured my entire role, giving me a team of eight direct reports (all known to be effective at implementation), providing financial resources, and (perhaps most importantly) redefining the scope of my responsibilities.

Things got a lot better, and we enjoyed two successful product launches in quick succession. Six months later, after our annual talent review, Greg said that the leadership team considers me a top-tier talent in the organization, with promotion potential for up to two levels above my current role.

Together, the organization and I debunked the myth of fit. I wasn't struggling because I didn't fit, but because I was in a role that wasn't structured for success.

Greg and Janet took time to understand the scope of the role, align resources and expectations, and set me up to succeed. And in turn, I utilized those resources and did my utmost to ensure their desired goals were met.

Unfortunately, Gretchen's experience is far more common than it should be—and the "Gretchens" of the world, as well as their companies, deserve better.

A lot rides on a typical leadership-level hire. In fact, many companies stake their futures on newly-placed CEOs and other senior leaders. So when those hires "go wrong," and a top leader fails, the pain is significant—for both the company and the New Leader. Yet the same onboarding mistakes are repeated. And New Leaders continue to derail.

In addition to the cost of replacement and the damage inflicted on their team, mistakes and missed opportunities can carry a multimillion dollar price tag.[1] When derailment occurs, the New Leader's demise is typically attributed to their "poor fit" with the organization and its culture.

Not surprisingly, we often hear clients talk about how they want to hire New Leaders who "fit" in their organization. The idea is understandably appealing to them—with an emphasis on fit, they believe they can increase certainty of New Leader success.

Distracted by a Glass-Slipper Mentality

Hiring Managers and HR Partners believe that someone who fits will settle in faster and more appropriately, with quicker ramp-up and higher eventual levels of performance. While it is important that New Leaders demonstrate behaviors and values that are relevant to the organization, it is only a portion of the foundation for future effectiveness and longevity.

This narrow way of thinking about selecting leaders promotes a "glass slipper" approach to hiring, and perpetuates the myth of fit. Many Hiring Managers or their HR Partners operate with the belief that only one person (or type of person) is a suitable candidate for that role. To that end, there is an ever-increasing array of assessment tools,[2] advertising ways for companies to ensure fit for new hires and screen out the "wrong" people (with the implication that if they don't pass the fit test, they will fail in their roles).

One of the issues with the fit perspective is that it has different meaning for different people. For many, fit could mean "be just like us," people who can meld flawlessly with their cultures. And since most companies want to perform better, this can be a tempting but mistaken notion.

- Too many similar people = too many people who think the same way.

- Too many people who think the same way = suppression of new ideas, or failure to challenge existing ideas.[3]

It also implies something unpleasant for those who are not considered mainstream—that as people with different work styles, genders, sexual orientations, experience bases, ethnicities, or skin colors, contributions will be marginalized (or simply not considered).[4]

In the book *Assimilating New Leaders: The Key to Executive Retention*, Diane Downey, Tom March, and Adena Berkman maintain that "fit isn't everything," and "the relative importance of different *kinds* of fit varies according to your organization's current needs. Someone who mirrors the current culture, values, and goals may fit in just fine as a direct replacement, but may therefore be less likely to contribute new ideas to emerging change efforts. It is important for a new leader to share the *core* values of an organization, and maybe even have alignment with its preferred work style. But fit is not simply a matter of similarity."[5]

Rather than accepting the "glass slipper" model, what if we define fit as the extent to which New Leaders behave in ways that are acceptable to their new peers and colleagues? If New Leaders respect their coworkers and their ways of doing things, they are likely to be more accepted by others, voice opinions more effectively, and become more influential. And it matters to their future a lot. In one study, coworker acceptance was one of the strongest predictors of New Leader turnover and performance.[6] The dynamics support a more situational way of thinking about leader transition. And that there is room in the organization for leaders of many types, provided they understand the behaviors foundational to their success.

Demystifying Fit

A compatible notion is the idea that fit is not solely the responsibility of the New Leader—that it is also the job of the organization to orchestrate the success of that person.[7] While this idea may take a bit of getting used to, it supports the premise that companies typically do a pretty good job of hiring people with the "potential to fit." Knowing that, why wouldn't those employers want to create more certainty by ensuring their new hires are truly set up for success?[8]

Starting a new job can be tough going, and it turns into a far more productive experience when the New Leader has assistance in their navigation. Anyone who has started a new role can attest to the organizational "maze" that must be negotiated as part of a successful transition.

The first dead-end can occur when the New Leader realizes post-hire that their role and company are not as described to them during the selection process. While difficult to accept, it is important for the New Leader to recognize what their role reality truly is, and adapt to it. The second potential dead-end appears when the New Leader has developed a nuanced understanding of the truly paradoxical nature of their transition. They see that they must:

- Bring about major change without making anyone unhappy or disrupting the organization.

- Be confident without being arrogant.

- Remain humble while leading a large team with a substantial budget (and power).

- Emphasize a focus on learning when they thought they needed to be actively demonstrating their worth.

While many New Leaders eventually demystify their transition, it often happens after a series of mistakes, retracing steps, and much frustration. It is only when they emerge on the other side of the maze that many New Leaders are seen as full-fledged members of the organizational culture. The purpose of leader onboarding is to support that successful navigation of the maze, gracefully recognizing and reconciling multiple challenges and paradoxes.

Finding a Balance: Sharing the Load

New Leader fit requires equilibrium. Downey, March, and Berkman assert that it is important to have commonalities between the New Leader and the organization. However, the authors state, "There should be adequate space for each to offer unique contributions and add value to the other. So, if the purpose of the hire is to push the organization in a new direction, finding the *proper* fit (not too close, not too far away) is critical."[9]

Rather than have "fit" be a throwaway explanation for success or derailment, doesn't it make sense for companies to have a better understanding of what contributes to desired New Leader outcomes, and why? Thus this book: if we can make the "failure of fit" be seen as what we really believe it to be—a failure to <u>cause</u> the fit of the New Leader—wouldn't everyone win? Companies retain valued leaders. New Leaders not only keep their jobs, but also ramp up faster and less painfully. Employees have more effective bosses and teams. And HR Partners get to attend to what they most want to do: retain and develop talent to drive stronger organizational performance.

If the challenges described sound familiar to you, perhaps the suggested actions that we have included at the end of each chapter may be helpful.

Your Keys to Overcoming the Myth of "Fit"

What the Hiring Manager can do.

- Be very clear about role expectations before, during and after the selection process.

- Avoid "glass slipper" thinking, and recognize that more than one kind of leader/way of leading can drive organizational success.

What the New Leader can do.

- Identify, and balance, your responses to the paradoxical nature of your transition.

- Be vigilant about, and adapt to, the cultural requirements for success.

What the HR Partner can do.

- Actively engage the Hiring Manager in the selection process, focusing on clear role expectations and true job requirements.

- Become a strong partner with the New Leader, building a "safe container" for confidential conversations about the paradoxical nature of their transition.

II

Overcoming the OnBoarding Paradox
A Balancing Act

When asked if they plan to provide onboarding support to new hires, many Hiring Managers say, "We picked the right person, so they don't need our help." What Hiring Managers often forget is just how nuanced and ever-changing a typical New Leader transition can (or needs to) be.[1] Even worse, the Hiring Manager may actually be expecting and saying things that increase the degree of difficulty for the New Leader—creating an onboarding paradox that is hard to fully recognize, and even harder to overcome.

Permanent solutions are elusive—perhaps the best they can do is create and sustain a dynamic equilibrium, which requires ongoing attention to balancing the paradoxes they face. Importantly, the risks associated with this universal problem can be mitigated if the New Leader and Hiring Manager are diligent. The eight paradoxes listed on the following pages represent the most common dilemmas that New Leaders may encounter.

> A leader is best when people barely know he exists, when his work is done, his aim fulfilled, they will say: we did it ourselves.
>
> Lao Tzu[2]

9

Paradox 1

Demonstrating competence	Seeking advice and help when needed

Many New Leaders have the mistaken notion that they need to immediately start demonstrating competence by jumping into the work and making quick decisions—targeting "low-hanging fruit." In most cases, this approach is not necessary or even helpful.

The risk (and prevalence) of this perspective is borne out by research, presented by Mark Van Buren and Todd Safferstone in their article "The Quick Wins Paradox," where they suggest that New Leaders who are too focused on quickly delivering results are at risk of exhibiting five potential derailment behaviors:

1. Make assumptions before understanding context.

2. Respond adversely to constructive feedback.

3. Become too fixated on details/minutiae.

4. Micromanage team members.

5. Intimidate or control others.

The same body of research also demonstrated that if New Leaders must deliver quick wins, they are more likely to be successful when including key others in collaborative decision-making and implementation.[3]

Although New Leaders commonly fret about "proving themselves," it is often the case that colleagues implicitly believe that the New Leader is qualified for the role. Interestingly, when the colleagues appraise competence, it is likely based on the degree to which New Leaders seek advice, listen, and learn, rather than what they say, know, and do. New Leaders who signal, through their inclusive behavior, that they want to become a long-term member of the organization are much more likely to build effective relationships, and thus gain needed knowledge and feedback.

Success mode:

- Enter the role with learning and developmental goals.

- Ask lots of questions in the first six to eight weeks, seek advice readily, and find value in what each person offers (even those who may not be performing well).

- Keep opinions internalized, and balance them against the advice of others.

Failure mode:

- Think and behave as though you are the smartest person in the room.

- Start transmitting ideas and opinions early and broadly.

- Go after "low-hanging fruit" without understanding why it has been left there untouched for everyone to see. If it's that significant, why hasn't anyone already taken action?

Paradox 2

Demonstrating value and becoming productive	Being patient

A corollary of Paradox 1, this item is a reminder to New Leaders that they are walking into an organization and team that has successfully existed (and performed) without them, often for many years. In order to be seen as productive, New Leaders must deliver what the organization truly needs from them, and resist the temptation to add value where none has been requested.

Leaders who want to have early impact run the risk of becoming goal-obsessed. According to Marshall Goldsmith and Mark

Reiter—leadership experts and authors of *What Got You Here Won't Get You There*—it is understandable that leaders generally want to set and pursue goals, "but it is often the root cause of annoying behavior. Goal obsession turns us into someone we shouldn't be."[4]

Importantly, true role requirements may not coincide with the understanding of the role that the New Leader developed during the recruitment process. Aligning these perceptions is crucially important. When New Leaders see their early role as one of discovery, and test their findings with their Hiring Manager, success ensues. At that point (typically about two months in role), the New Leader stands a much better chance of productively contributing to the organization.

Success mode:

- Resist the temptation to make immediate changes (or foreshadow future changes), even when the organization may be struggling.

- Include others from a broad cross-section of the organization in the search for understanding—particularly in identification of root causes of performance issues.

- Think carefully about how to ask questions in a way that leads to open and honest conversation.

Failure mode:

- Come in with the answers without having asked the questions—being heroic may not be called for, and can create friction in the New Leader's relationships.

- Make decisions without considering the impact on other areas of the operation or organization.

- Change things without including others in the decision, or before truly understanding why what you're changing doesn't already work.

Paradox 3

Implementing change	Respecting the history and culture of the organization

Many, if not most, New Leaders are hired to bring about change—sometimes enormous change. And some, feeling they have a clear mandate, begin implementing change from the time they walk in the door. It's important to remember Newton's third law states that for every action, there is an equal and opposite reaction. New Leaders who try to quickly execute change without completely understanding the context are likely to experience blowback and find it very difficult going, even if the change is logical and the need may even be obvious to others.

Effective New Leaders understand that a logical change first creates an emotional reaction[5]—and that the emotional reaction is usually tied to the employee's desire to be able to continue to drive needed results. While it is tempting to identify reluctant employees as "change resistant," it is much wiser for the New Leader to ask themselves what they have failed to do to help each team member understand and embrace a new way of working.

Success mode:

- Ask lots of questions about past performance, change efforts, and reasons for success or failure of those efforts.

- Try to foresee how needed change may (temporarily) disrupt performance, and acknowledge that expectation to those affected by change. Then support them as they adapt.

- Understand how the organizational culture is likely to support and/or thwart change efforts, and develop strategies for success.

Failure mode:

- Assume that because there is a change mandate, employees should embrace the change without question.

- Take action in a way that is contrary to cultural norms within the organization, such as failing to be inclusive, being too aggressive, or not respecting those who will be most impacted by the change.

- Believe that earlier failed change was because of the person leading it, rather than the organizational context or other constraints.

Paradox 4

Being decisive	Going slowly enough to validate decisions

New Leaders understandably feel pressure to diagnose problems and take action early in their tenure. Their Hiring Manager, peers and colleagues are observing their transition and actively forming judgments about their likely future viability. It is not wrong for New Leaders to be decisive—but they must consider the method and timing of their decision-making.

In any New Leader transition, situations may arise that require responsiveness or quick action. Unless it is an emergency, it is still advisable to reach out to a variety of trusted colleagues to learn about historical precedents, and think through the potential implications of the decision to be taken. In his book, *The First 90 Days*, Michael Watkins recommends speaking at length with those who can offer a perspective on the New Leader's operation. He also suggests that those key stakeholders can include both internal colleagues, as well as external partners (vendors or customers, for example). That insight can provide additional grounding.[6]

In the case of an emergency, the New Leader will be more effective by staying calm, sharing information with colleagues as it becomes known, trying to understand the situation's impact on others, and focusing on how to lead a diverse group through uncertainty.[7]

Success mode:

- Couch decisions in information gleaned through interactions with those who better-understand the organization.

- When possible, make decisions inclusively/collaboratively.

- See situations as complex and/or nuanced, and without an obvious easy fix.

Failure mode:

- Make decisions in a vacuum.

- Base actions on the perceived likelihood that they will impress others.

- View situations as "black and white" with obvious answers.

Paradox 5

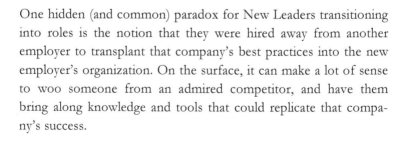

Drawing on past experience	Accurately understanding new realities

One hidden (and common) paradox for New Leaders transitioning into roles is the notion that they were hired away from another employer to transplant that company's best practices into the new employer's organization. On the surface, it can make a lot of sense to woo someone from an admired competitor, and have them bring along knowledge and tools that could replicate that company's success.

However, what worked in one company may not work in another—because of differences in organizational structure, culture, or approach to work processes. Even in smaller operations, placing the responsibility for transforming the organization onto the shoulders of one person can spell their doom.

One Leader's Experience

I was hired to lead the Marketing function in my new company, based on the award-winning digital work done at a previous employer. The thing that surprised me most about the job was being quickly (and repeatedly) advised not to talk about my past experiences. I had to spend a lot of time listening and learning about my new team and company, and even then found I could only generically refer to my previous digital experience. It made me wonder whether or not they wanted me to bring the change I was hired to drive. It was frustrating and demoralizing.

Somewhat counter-intuitively, to get others to accept and use the knowledge and expertise provided by a New Leader, that individual must first study and understand the organization they are joining. They also need to demonstrate a deep understanding of, and respect for, the operation as it existed on their hire date. Only then will others be truly curious about, and open to, best practices offered by the New Leader that might drive better performance.

Success mode:

- When asked how something was done at the old employer, demur and acknowledge you need to learn more before suggesting solutions.

- Ask lots of questions about internal/existing best practices, including those from other areas of the organization.

- Involve your new team in assessing the operation's effectiveness and making recommendations, and only then share your previous best practices more generically.

Failure mode:

- Draw heavily on solutions (and reference) used in your last job, and fail to recognize the differences between your old and new organization and role.

- Get blinded by the change mandate, and opt to implement your own best practices rather than taking time to learn from new colleagues.

- Exclude others from the search for best practices.

Paradox 6

Making improvements	Not devaluing what already exists

▲

Hiring Managers make things harder when they ask New Leaders to fix things that are broken, or improve performance in specific ways—and expect it to be done without causing pain, discomfort or disruption. (Some employers even sheepishly admit that they want the New Leader to fix things without causing any change.) Again, while an obvious, logical reason may exist for needed improvements, it is the <u>how</u> of tackling those improvements that will sow the seeds of the New Leader's ultimate success or failure.

In most cases, New Leaders do encounter broken processes that include some effective (though perhaps not cutting-edge) elements. To minimize disruption, the New Leader should consider fixing only those elements that truly don't work, rather than unveiling a splashy transformation that requires a completely transformed way of doing business. While this approach may not be as attention-getting in the broader organization, it respects the needs of the employees to continue to perform (at least as well as they did before the New Leader came on board). The same thought process can be applied when sizing up talent. New Leaders who come in and pronounce their team completely inadequate (and then quickly trade them out for colleagues from their former employer) can never truly comprehend the cost of such actions.[8] Continuity is disrupted, knowledge is lost, morale plummets, influential relationships are severed, and it can take a year or more for these transplants to perform at full effectiveness.

Success mode:

- Enlist the team in a broad search for existing best practices, and retain and expand those practices wherever possible.

- Include team members in assessing areas needing improvement, and allow their influence in decisions made and actions taken.

- Ensure there is a solid business reason provided for each improvement taken on.

Failure mode:

- Fail to recognize existing best practices, instead focusing on all that is wrong with the operation.

- Invest most effort in the sub-function or area you know most about, dive too deep, and cause others to feel resentful, fearful or devalued.

- Make a "clean sweep" of the team without considering how the context could have caused previous underperformance.

Paradox 7

Building important relationships	Not being seen as overly political or having favorites

In most organizations, a New Leader's long-term survival depends on creation of successful relationships. Colleagues serve as sounding boards, and can evaluate the potential implications of actions being considered. In general, they also afford access to needed knowledge and feedback. If New Leaders wish to move initiatives forward, they must rapidly develop a sense of "the lay of the land." However, a barrier to acquiring organizational knowledge through relationships is that information is rarely shared through formal channels of communication.

A research-based article, "Harnessing the Power of Informal Employee Networks" by Lowell Bryan, Eric Matson, and Leigh Weiss, supports this notion. They observe, "As we used surveys and e-mail analysis to map the way employees actually exchange information and knowledge, we concluded that the formal structures of companies, as manifested in their organizational charts, don't explain how most of their real day-to-day work gets done."[9]

It is important for the New Leader to understand the needs and perspectives of their broad base of colleagues, and to appropriately meet those needs. The key is to take a balanced approach to office politics—New Leaders who get drawn into conflict between individuals or areas make themselves vulnerable to manipulation and reputational damage.

New Leaders benefit from remaining detached and trying to understand the motives driving others' behavior. Without appearing skeptical, sizing up what each person may be angling for can keep New Leaders above the fray. Early in our onboarding work, one astute client remembered, "I've learned to be cautious in interacting with the first person who stops by my office. It has been my experience that this friendly-seeming behavior isn't what it seems."

To successfully navigate a political climate, establishing, and maintaining, healthy interpersonal boundaries must be a priority while being aware of personal blind spots. New Leaders are well-served to focus on being balanced and fair in decision-making, and remaining neutral in contentious situations (while validating the importance of both perspectives where possible).[10] This neutrality will make the New Leader a trusted colleague who is able to rise above the fray.

Success mode:

- Invest in relationships—think beyond the initial "meet and greet."

- Ask questions about organizational norms, how to get things done, and what to avoid doing.

- Avoid getting drawn into active participation in contentious conversations.

Failure mode:

- Engage in negative conversations about new colleagues.

- Interact primarily with those most like yourself, and seem disinterested in the nuances of relationship-building.

- Take sides—coming down firmly in one camp, especially early in your tenure.

Paradox 8

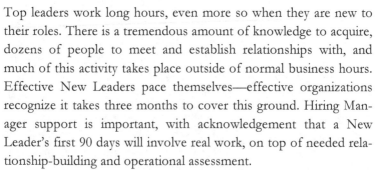

| Giving it your all | Not ignoring personal needs |

Top leaders work long hours, even more so when they are new to their roles. There is a tremendous amount of knowledge to acquire, dozens of people to meet and establish relationships with, and much of this activity takes place outside of normal business hours. Effective New Leaders pace themselves—effective organizations recognize it takes three months to cover this ground. Hiring Manager support is important, with acknowledgement that a New Leader's first 90 days will involve real work, on top of needed relationship-building and operational assessment.

When starting a new role, two kinds of personal challenges often surface. The first is that a New Leader with a spouse and children may need to take up temporary residence in their new location while the family stays behind to complete the school year, sell their home and prepare for their move. This can be a time of stress for the family, but also great opportunity for the New Leader, as they may be able to work long hours without a negative impact on their home life. The key is to do so without creating a habit (and expectations) of working those same hours, or working the same way, once the family is in place.

A second concern about the personal needs of the New Leader centers around the importance of building routines that will sustain them in the long-run. Regular exercise and sufficient rest and recreation increase a New Leader's energy reserves, as does connecting themselves and their family in the broader community (whether through relatives and friends, sports, a place of worship, volunteer work, or the pursuit of a meaningful hobby). This connectedness will help the New Leader and their family respond resiliently to the natural ups and downs of leader transition.

Success mode:

- Attend to job requirements without foregoing the needs of loved ones.

- Stay fit for the demands of the transition, whether from work or home, by taking good care of yourself (and enjoying life).

- Focus on the needs of the family, and become rooted in one or more communities that are meaningful to everyone.

Failure mode:

- Be driven by ambition, fear or anxiety, and unable to draw boundaries between work and time spent in activities that could "recharge your batteries."

- Pay little attention to the needs to your family during relocation.

- Overlook the value of becoming connected to your new community, risking isolation and burnout.

One Leader's Experience

In my last job, I was placed in a corporate staff position after holding a series of field-based operational roles—with the idea that it would round out my leadership experience and make me more promotable. Going in, it was clear that I'd have to rely more on influencing others instead of driving performance through my team. That was a rough transition for me—pretty humbling.

The hardship I <u>didn't</u> expect was that when we moved in the middle of the school year, our children instantly hated our new neighborhood, school system, and city. We had made three successful moves before, but they were younger then. Them being teenagers was a game-changer. They had a hard time making friends, and missed their old ones. And my wife was the one they lashed out at, because I was working long hours. The worst part of all was that I found I couldn't talk with her about the disappointment and stress in my own job, because I didn't want to push her over the edge with everything else she was dealing with. Neither one of us got enough sleep or exercise, and didn't have much fun.

My stress multiplied, as did my isolation. At the end of the school year, my family said they wanted to move back to our old city, and asked that I commute home on weekends. That wasn't acceptable to me, so I looked for, and found, a job closer to my family. Looking back, I think we could have planned and handled things a lot better, and probably could have made it work. But we didn't.

Success in managing onboarding paradoxes requires maintaining self-awareness, and adapting to the new environment. Every New Leader brings to their role ways of working that have driven past success, and it's important to step back and understand how the new environment may require changes in behavior. Goldsmith and Reiter encourage self-reflection to address the paradoxical nature of leadership, stating, "Beliefs that carried us *here* may be holding us back in our quest to go *there*."[11]

Your Keys to Balancing the OnBoarding Paradox

What the Hiring Manager can do.

❦ Articulate clear role expectations, then recognize and communicate about the paradoxical nature of the New Leader's transition. Help the New Leader understand that the paradoxes will continue, and will likely shift over time.

❦ Work to "fly air cover" for the New Leader when the competing challenges of the transition get out of balance (and don't wait for the New Leader to seek you out for help—checking in is part of your role).

What the New Leader can do.

❦ Remember that it is your job to learn and appreciate the history of your new organization, and build relationships—these actions will foster your long-term success. Don't feel like you need to know everything, or be all things to all people. Ask questions and demonstrate respect, trying to learn what other people know and have done.

❦ Remain humble—resist the temptation to engage in heroics. And make your transition about people and topics other than you.

What the HR Partner can do.

❦ Help the New Leader navigate the internal workings of the organization by making introductions and sharing insights. Also, assist the New Leader in understanding the tone that the organizational conversation is taking, and provide support and balance in that discussion.

❦ Check in with the New Leader to identify any paradoxical experiences they are having, and help them resolve those.

III

OnBoarding As a Risk Management Process

There are few Hiring Managers who don't feel some anxiety when making key hires.[1] Those worries are compounded for senior management hires—these strategically important roles often require change leadership, accompanied by significant performance pressure. And while the Hiring Manager and their HR Partner may have assessed and vetted candidates, and even made what they consider to be the ideal hire, the New Leader's success is not a foregone conclusion.[2] In many ways, the thinking behind the successful hiring and onboarding of a New Leader resembles the risk management strategies employed by those same companies. This definition illustrates the basic premise:

risk man·age·ment
n. (In business) the forecasting and evaluation of financial risks together with the identification of procedures to avoid or minimize their impact.[3]

Executives typically underestimate the complexity and challenges associated with placing a New Leader in a role, often with serious consequences for them and organization. While the organization may be excited about the appointment, it is important that work be done behind the scenes to identify and manage the risks associated with that hire.[4]

25

One of the paradoxes for New Leaders is that companies hire people in whom they have confidence; and because they believe in the Leader's abilities, do nothing to support onboarding transitions. Unfortunately, many New Leaders mistake this lack of guidance as blanket permission to lead as they please.

When discussing this phenomenon from the perspective of a New Leader, authors of *Leadership Passages*—David Dotlich, James Noel, and Norman Walker—state, "Their previous success frequently makes them closed to new learning. As a result, top people join companies believing they have been hired to make change, improve performance, and rewrite history, and conclude that they must know everything necessary to succeed. And then they fail."[5] Every leader transition carries with it some form of risk, a fact companies (and New Leaders) may fail to recognize.

Over the years, our clients have found increasing value in treating leader onboarding as a risk management process. Some of the risks inherent in the transition are about the Leader—such as being a first-time general manager. In *The Leadership Pipeline*, Ram Charan, Stephen Drotter, and James Noel state that those who advance to a business management position from the functional management level often "feel that they're 'going it alone'—they're receiving much less guidance from their boss."[6]

Others risk factors are a function of the organization and the role itself—such as unreasonably inflated standards for performance, conflicting expectations from multiple bosses, or the presence of rivals. Whatever the genesis, the risks present threats to New Leader effectiveness and survival.

Our client research indicates that while some risk factors may weigh more heavily than others, the sheer number of them is in itself a strong predictor of longevity and effective performance (or, conversely, derailment and turnover). The greater the number of risks, the more problematic the transition. Clients typically retain *Leader OnBoarding* coaches to manage and mitigate transition risks when the total number exceeds six.

One client faced some daunting challenges in her transition. How many risk factors can you spot?

- Katherine was promoted from SVP, Marketing to become the publicly-traded consumer products company's first female President.

- Her predecessor became CEO and Chairman—remaining active in the operations of the business—and managed M&A strategy development.

- When the search for her replacement failed to identify a suitable candidate, Katherine also continued to lead the Marketing function for nearly six months.

- Katherine relocated her family (a spouse and three teens) from Manhattan to suburbs in a nearby state, and left behind a trusted pediatric cardiologist who had treated their daughter's congenital heart defect since birth.

- A rival for the role was so unhappy about her promotion that he accepted a job offer from a competitor. At least two of her now-direct reports had been interested in the role, but were not even asked to interview for it.

- Katherine became the sponsor of a company-wide performance improvement initiative that included aspects of LEAN management, and more aggressive productivity and performance goals. (This represents her first exposure to LEAN principles.)

- Within three months of her promotion, the company purchased its number three competitor, which was a family-owned business based in Europe.

- Five months later, the newly-expanded company was taken private and purchased by an equity firm.

Would you want Katherine's job? Why or why not? In the case presented above, Katherine faced 10 or more transition risk factors. Fortunately, her Hiring Manager understood the breadth and complexity of the challenges, and put aggressive onboarding support in place. He also broadly communicated the expectation that the company's performance could stay flat, or even dip, in Katherine's first year due to myriad operational and strategic changes.

Though the case represented on the previous page was an extreme example of risky leader transition, most high-level hires face unrealistic or misaligned expectations, as well as other internal challenges. So why don't most Hiring Managers and their organizations do something about recognizing and mitigating New Leader transition risk? Companies may resist a risk management focus for a number of reasons:

- Hiring Managers lack awareness of the hazards, or the role they play in New Leader success (or failure).

- They've obscured some of the risk during the recruiting process in order to attract the very best talent available (and do not wish to acknowledge it post-hire).

- There are legitimate concerns about highlighting multiple risk factors post-hire, worrying that such a focus can increase New Leader anxiety, and make them self-conscious in an unhelpful way.

- They see identifying risk (and taking steps to mitigate it) as a "vote of no confidence" in the New Leader, suggesting that someone who needs transition support is "damaged goods."

One client has a best practice of identifying risk factors upfront, and then mitigating transition-related risk throughout an onboarding coaching engagement. Treating onboarding risk management with intent, using appropriate tools, and gaining support from the Hiring Manager and HR Partner ideally starts before the New Leader's first day in the role.

While there may be some problematic aspects of the role and/or transition that need to be pointed out and worked through with the New Leader, it is important to provide the right amount (and type) of information to maximize their effectiveness and minimize focus on potential danger. Plowing headlong into repeated risk management discussions is akin to telling a golfer to "not hit your tee shot into the water hazard." And we all know, of course, this advice greatly increases the likelihood of putting the ball directly into the water. Instead, consider using the onboarding process to proactively identify and address risks. This can be accomplished by:

- Presenting candidates for the role with accurate, complete information about the culture, the state of operations, and challenges faced.[7]

- Defining the role as thoroughly as possible, making expectations clear during the selection process, and revisiting regularly thereafter.[8]

- Giving the New Leader tools that help them analyze the needs of their extended network of stakeholders, and align their expectations.

- Emphasizing learning about the company, its business units, and functions/geographies.

- Providing the New Leader with early, comprehensive feedback about the effectiveness of their transition to date.

Our job as coaches and advisors to senior leadership is to help them confidently weather the challenges they face, providing support and tools to foster more effective and faster transitions. And, at the core of that process is the identification, and mitigation, of the risk factors that threaten or slow their success.

Through applied research, *Leader OnBoarding* has identified nearly 20 major risk factors that may influence New Leader transitions. Some are addressed in this chapter.

- Which areas are of concern in your (or your New Leader's) situation?

- How are you managing and/or mitigating those risks?

Your Keys to Identifying and Mitigating OnBoarding Risks

What the Hiring Manager can do.

- Articulate clear role expectations, and listen for lack of alignment with those of dotted-line managers, or other key stakeholders. Ensure that you and the New Leader have a similar understanding of their job—expect it to change and evolve over time.

- Work with an onboarding expert to identify the risk factors inherent in the New Leader's transition, and put an aggressive action plan in place to mitigate or ameliorate risk wherever possible.

What the New Leader can do.

- Don't assume that the job you accepted will have the same responsibilities as the job you experience post-hire. Check in weekly with your Hiring Manager to ensure that deliverables are aligned with role expectations, and listen carefully for inconsistencies in the assumptions held by others (dotted-line managers, other key stakeholders).

- Recognize that building successful relationships, and keeping a focus on learning and respect, will enhance your effectiveness, no matter the challenges you face.

What the HR Partner can do.

- Work with the Hiring Manager to scope the role correctly pre-hire, and transparently communicate expectations and deliverables to each final candidate. Continue this conversation with the Hiring Manager and New Leader for several months post-hire.

- Build your own onboarding knowledge base and capacity— be a thought partner to the New Leader as they learn about the company, operations, team, and culture. Act as a neutral sounding board, remaining wary of overly-influencing the

New Leader's perceptions. Ask a variety of questions about their experiences and lessons learned, and make few declarative statements about their transition.

IV

Why Role Clarity Is So Important—and Difficult—To Achieve

It should be simple—after a thoughtful selection process, a company hires a great candidate. That New Leader comes in and does a stellar job without stumbling, delights key stakeholders and performs at a high level.

But it isn't simple. The reality is that many New Leaders struggle, often mightily, to become effective in their new roles. They all too frequently fail, and pay a high personal and professional price—fired from their roles, their reputations tarnished. And the employer is out hundreds of thousands of dollars (even millions, for certain key hires).[1] Their teams also endure a variety of hardships, from working on the wrong things to alienating colleagues and suffering low morale that can double their own turnover.[2]

New Leaders Don't Truly Understand Their Jobs

After studying and supporting executive-level transitions for over 20 years, we have come to believe that the role and operation the New Leaders thought they were signing up for are <u>always</u> different than what they end up with.

This understanding gap can have multiple causes, and can hobble New Leaders—especially when others interpret the gap as evidence that they don't "get it." Lack of role clarity is a significant contributor to New Leader ineffectiveness. In fact, our client research indicates that the failure to establish and maintain role clarity is the number one predictor of New Leader derailment. Here's what's sad—these painful problems can be prevented and treated, leading to faster ramp-up, higher performance, and longer tenure.

Instead of attributing New Leader misfires to poor "fit," or blaming them for their failure, hiring organizations can recognize that they jointly shoulder responsibility for driving New Leader role clarity. Through proactive partnership, together the organizations and the New Leaders coordinate "fit," achieving alignment and success.

Lack of Role Clarity Has Many Causes

Many leadership experts address the importance of role clarity in the work of leaders, in general. According to Ram Charan, Stephen Drotter, and James Noel, authors of *The Leadership Pipeline*, "This factor [role clarity] is paramount in a business environment that is increasingly ambiguous, paradoxical, complex, and volatile."[3] Also, onboarding experts Diane Downey, Tom March, and Adena Berkman, state in the book *Assimilating New Leaders*, "A big source of confusion as the new leader assimilates is lack of role clarity. Who does what? What are the gray areas? What is the work flow? What needs to be changed?"[4] Getting answers to these and other questions becomes a New Leader's most important work in their early days.

New Leaders must recognize that both the business context and others' behavior can create (and exacerbate) confusion around their role. Gaining role clarity is like putting together a large puzzle—it takes thought, time, and use of reference points. Gaining understanding of root causes is essential, and they are varied.

The Recruitment Process Obscures Role Realities

The first step in the process of creating misalignment of expectations often begins with the recruitment process. Companies work hard to attract top talent for leadership roles. The business environment is volatile, the competition has become more aggressive, and employers want to win. This ups the ante—it becomes more important to hire highly capable leaders who can drive immediate results.

In many ways, recruitment is like a romance—the company sets its sights on the best candidates, and works to make itself attractive to them. To get those top candidates, companies often create campaigns to woo them—sometimes targeting those who are "out of their league." This over-reaching has the potential to blur the lines in the selection process, where needed facts are omitted, and truths burnished to be more appealing. This failure to properly equip candidates is precisely where trouble begins.

- Candidates are flown in, wined and dined, and shown the most appealing aspects of the company's culture, role and operation. The wooing doesn't end there—they may get home and to find flowers on their doorstep, or an assortment of the company's marquee products.

- While some employers simply want to highlight their best features, others actively suppress information that would stop candidates from even considering the role. However, trying to optimize their own outcomes at the expense of candidate understanding is a "win/lose" proposition. The organization may get their top candidate, but the company's credibility will be tarnished when the New Leader develops a true understanding of what they signed up for. Tricking them into taking the role simply increases resentment and the likelihood they will leave.

- People aspiring for the role wish to present their best selves, but they are at a disadvantage because the selection process focuses on exploring only what the employer believes they need to know about the candidate. An effective selection process happens only when both employer and candidate exercise mutual transparency, which lays the foundation for a successful match and ongoing partnership.

The employer can—through interviews, background checks, and pre-hire assessments—do a pretty good job of sizing up the candidates, as well as their potential to succeed in the company culture. Unfortunately, the candidates have a more limited ability to understand what is real about the company, role, and operation presented to them. They can do their due diligence through research and reputation, ask questions in the interview process, and negotiate the boundaries of a role. Some potential sources of misunderstanding include:

- Typically, the true nature of the New Leaders' responsibilities isn't fully apparent to them until after they start the job.

- Some candidates have "selective hearing"—choosing to understand the positives of the role while discounting factors that could make their own success difficult to achieve.

- Others are so desperate to land a job that they don't even really care about what the role and expectations are—they just want to get hired.

As a result, for many New Leaders, accepting a role can be a little like an arranged marriage—they make a significant commitment with limited insight into their future (and the challenges they face). As time passes, if they remain vigilant, they become aware that things are very different than they expected. And then, if it's not already too late, they have to decide whether to adapt or leave.

The Role Changes between the Offer Acceptance and Start Date

And the change is often not for the better. The search process can be long—often nine to twelve months lapse between the first conversation and the New Leader's eventual start date. In the meantime, the job itself can morph into something entirely different. Some possible scenarios include the following.

1. The role or operation gets redefined through reorganization.

    ▪ Though a fairly commonplace practice, when reorganization happens between the acceptance and start dates, and hasn't been adequately communicated, the New Leader is essentially starting a job they didn't interview for or accept.

    ▪ The New Leader also may not realize that the role is being completely recast, and fail to adapt to new realities.

2. The Hiring Manager leaves, and the New Leader now has to reconfirm the job, its scope, deliverables, and resources with his or her new boss.

    ▪ This change often involves major redefinition of the New Leader's role, and it's crucial that the changes are recognized and adapted to.

    ▪ Unfortunately, it sometimes take a few months for that replacement to step in, leaving the New Leader in limbo and uncertain how to proceed. Their lack of direction can create broader, negative opinions of New Leader capability and viability.

3. A shift in strategic direction, even if based on very real need, can profoundly impact the New Leader's role and opinion about the organization.

    ▪ It's common for workload, funding and staffing shifts to follow, while New Leaders become accountable for delivering the same (or more significant) results with fewer resources.

    ▪ In the worst cases, New Leaders find themselves to be not well-suited for, nor happy about, the new strategy and its execution. They either have to choose to adapt, scramble to develop capacity, or face the eventual prospect of moving on to a different employer.

Given the various potential causes of role shift, New Leaders would be best-served if they started the role assuming that their new role has already changed, and work to understand the dynamic nature of their responsibilities throughout the onboarding process.

New Leader Doesn't "Right Size" Hiring Manager's Unrealistically High Expectations

New Leaders should beware the Hiring Manager who is looking for a hero to fill the role. Some phrases are giveaways—such as, "We're hiring this leader to single-handedly turn the company around," or, "In this job, the New Leader will fundamentally change our culture." Even the old standby, "do more with less" suggests a misalignment of the demands of the role and resources available—and the smart candidate will investigate thoroughly.

Best practice for New Leaders is to resist the temptation to let the Hiring Manager place them on a pedestal, recognizing that it is both unrealistic and likely to cause hard feelings among new colleagues. The earlier New Leaders can nip this misguided approach in the bud, the better.

There is a cost to taking others' expectations literally and not negotiating through the accountabilities and barriers. Setting unrealistic performance targets can lead to what Marshall Goldsmith and Mark Reiter call "goal obsession," and that can place certain leaders in the position of becoming "cheaters." In others words, being put in the compromising position of delivering on unrealistic expectations can encourage New Leaders to resort to unethical practices.[5]

The New Leader Fails to Align Others' Inappropriate or Contradictory Expectations

Every New Leader needs to remember that their role is actually the sum total of the expectations held by key others—expectations that can be inherently paradoxical. Role conflict can be problematic—and destructive. No matter how unrealistic, any expectation gaps that aren't reconciled early in their tenure quickly become the generally recognized definition of the New Leader's role.

Some less-principled new colleagues may capitalize on the ambiguity of the transition to either engage in a "land grab," or to foist their own responsibilities off onto the New Leader or their team. The New Leader will benefit from remaining vigilant in the search for, and reconciliation of, contradictory and inappropriate role expectations. Forever.

Recognizing That They Don't Know What They Need to Know

Whether joining from the outside or making an internal move, one source of New Leader risk is that they don't know what they need to know about the role and work itself. This is particularly true when they experience a jump in job scope—especially for first-time general managers. David Dotlich, James Noel, and Norman Walker address this notion of insecurity in *Leadership Passages*, stating, "It's a shock to discover that you're unqualified in some way for a task or position you've been given."[6]

Although this challenge may stem from inaccurate role description during the interview process, it is more often an unfortunate artifact of the New Leader's lack of preparation for the role. The quality of the selection process is key. Companies with highly effective talent acquisition and management processes are much less likely to hire or promote a Leader who is not fully ready to perform at the next level. They provide a thorough selection process for all candidates, plus assessment, training, and real-world developmental preparation for internal leaders.

Ways to Help New Leaders Truly Understand All Aspects of Their Roles

Though vexing problems can stem from New Leaders "not getting it," there are solutions to the fairly common experiences described above. Organizations can mitigate or improve these situations, in most cases, by:

- Being truthful/transparent with candidates about the company, role, and operation before they accept the position. It may feel risky to do so, but research clearly demonstrates the value of realistic job previews in driving New Leader satisfaction and retention.[7]

- Structuring their onboarding process to repeatedly revisit, and reconfirm, the scope and deliverables for the New Leader's role, examine what may have changed, and respond to the varied expectations held by significant stakeholders to the operation.

- Performing a *Culture Snapshot* (see page 171) assessment, which helps the New Leader develop a rapid, comprehensive understanding of the operation they now lead. Armed with these insights into what they've really gotten themselves into, the New Leader can take the right actions, in the right way, and at the right time.

- Providing the New Leader with *LevelSet: Early Feedback* (see page 171) about the effectiveness of their transition within the first eight weeks in the role. It will deepen their understanding of others' expectations for them, their role, and their operation—before it's too late to "get it."

New Leaders <u>Can</u> Establish and Maintain Role Clarity

Most importantly, New Leaders must remember that role definition should be a high priority for them—even before day one. Since roles change over time, they need to see it as an ongoing effort, conducted in concert with key stakeholders, though hopefully not as all-encompassing as in the early days of a new job. If such ambiguity is a concern, New Leaders should consider some of these strategies to bring roles into clear focus.

- Recognize that <u>every</u> role ends up being different than communicated during the selection process, and accept that adaptation will be key to future success.

- Be honest with yourself about the deliverables and skills required for success in the new job—before you accept it.[8]

- Ask the Hiring Manager about expectations and deliverables—frequently.

- "Ride the circuit" with key stakeholders, and explicitly request their understanding of the role and its history, past performance and their operation's expectations.

- Listen for disconnects and evidence that others' understanding of the role isn't as you expected.

- Take a developmental approach to the transition, recognizing which of your skills require ongoing cultivation to support long-term success in role.

- Get feedback—both formally and informally, to learn how others perceive your operation, as well as your own transition efforts.

In short, New Leaders need to understand that they don't have fixed job descriptions—that their roles continually evolve and they must readily adapt. Priorities and expectations will be in conflict, and New Leaders must recognize the contradictions and manage them. Strong relationships and frequent communication will help New Leaders stay aware of others' expectations and gain crucial feedback and knowledge.

And while New Leaders need support from others in order to establish and maintain role clarity, it is ultimately their own fundamental responsibility. Why would they leave it to chance?

Your Keys to Achieving and Maintaining New Leader Role Clarity

What the Hiring Manager can do.

1 Communicate transparently throughout the selection process—about the organizational culture, role expectations, and current challenges. Ask your candidates to mirror back their

understanding of the job, and help them adjust where needed. Be candid in your responses to questions, and admit when you may not know the answer to a question.

♟ In your first several meetings with the New Leader, review your expectations for the role. If they have another manager (dotted-line, for example), try to identify and reconcile the potential areas of expectation divergence or role conflict. Set the understanding that the role definition will be an ongoing process. Keep the conversation going, so the New Leader can understand, and adapt to, evolving expectations.

What the New Leader can do.

♟ Actively participate in the selection process—testing your understanding of the role and operation, asking clarifying questions, and assessing whether you truly want the job that is being described to you. Challenge yourself to listen for what the role actually is, and not what you want it to be. It's very easy to miss the nuances potential employers may communicate. Take note of what you <u>don't</u> hear—whether it's about specific performance expectations, sources of potential funding, or staffing levels in your operation.

♟ Recognize when you find yourself having energy for one major aspect of the role, but not another. You will be held accountable for the role in its entirety, and will benefit from a disciplined approach to its implementation. Check in frequently with your Hiring Manager and any dotted-line managers post-hire, to achieve and maintain alignment in their expectations for you and your operation.

What the HR Partner can do.

♟ Be a strong partner in the selection process, and also in the New Leader's onboarding. Work closely with the Hiring Manager to properly articulate the role. Communicate transparently to the New Leader about the role and expectations, and don't shy away from tackling tough conversations—

better now than facing a bigger problem later. Listen for disconnects and wishful thinking about the role, then recognize them early and tackle them directly. Support the New Leader to identify and fill in skill gaps.

⚡ Remember that you will be an important source of role clarity for the New Leader—focus on building a strong relationship with transparent communication. Your goal: to be the person they come to (a sounding board and feedback provider) when they encounter contradictory role expectations. Listen for their concerns and frustrations (and address them wherever possible).

V

The Myth of the Flawless Outsider

Why is it that so many companies exhibit a strong preference for recruiting external hires to fill key leadership roles?

Much has been written about the challenge and complexity facing today's leaders. Emerging technologies, aggressive competition, rapid change and escalation of consumer expectations all combine to make leadership a riskier proposition than ever before.[1] The pressure on leaders to drive results can be extreme, and it is magnified when they step into new roles.

Filling these roles can present a daunting challenge for employers, as circumstances demand breadth of leadership capabilities, depth of technical skills, and the wisdom required for successful navigation of an entirely new landscape. As companies explore the pool of candidates for these crucial roles, they often make the mistake of overlooking the internal talent they have cultivated.

Leadership experts Ram Charan, Stephen Drotter, and James Noel, observe, "Just about every major organization is attempting to hire 'stars,' offering enormous compensation to entice the best and the brightest." But, they also warn, "These overly aggressive, sometimes desperate attempts to recruit outsiders suggest that the leadership pipeline is inadequate."[2]

Are these rational, data-based hiring decisions that favor hiring external candidates, or are the decision-makers falling prey to hidden biases that could prevent them from placing the right person in the role? If so, then at what cost?

We call this blind spot the myth of the flawless outsider, and it has several components:

- **A "plug and play" mentality**

  The Hiring Manager wants to appoint someone who has already successfully navigated a situation similar to the one the New Leader must face in this role. Common during periods of organizational transition or difficulty, this way of thinking ignores the time, complexity, and nuance required for an external hire to become a credible, full-fledged organizational citizen and leader.

- **The hero complex**

  There is a natural tendency to cast a tough role with a heroic figure—someone who can be placed on a pedestal by the organization. Companies like to hire "superstars"—leaders who walk with a swagger.[3] The risk in this kind of thinking includes the possibility of backlash against a New Leader who goes it alone in order to be heroic, tackles change too aggressively, or buys into seeking (and enjoying) the limelight. Resentment festers, and the New Leader's efforts could be undermined.

- **Overlooking the familiar**

  A focus on the need for significant talent and thought leadership may encourage Hiring Managers to overlook the familiar strengths of internal candidates, and (instead) concentrate on their relative weaknesses. People and organizations tend to have long memories about the failings of individuals—from an early gaffe made at a board meeting to a conflict with a powerful colleague. This problem can be compounded in an organization that doesn't provide timely, relevant, corrective feedback. And it compromises a Hiring Manager's ability to accurately size up the full complement of internal candidates' capabilities.

▪ **Unrealistic perception of the external candidate**
All other things being equal, a lack of familiarity with external candidates means their résumés tend to look "rosier" than the facts known about existing colleagues. The selection process typically doesn't dive deep enough to foster full understanding of the career ups and downs (and personal idiosyncrasies) of external candidates—information that may not be gained until well after their start date.

▪ **Ignoring relevant facts and data**
Finally, some in the hiring process tend to devalue available information, and fail to evaluate candidates on all relevant criteria during interviews. Many leaders pride themselves on using their "gut instincts" about candidates, and can downplay (or under-weight) the data gained from structured interviewing and pre-hire assessments.

The costs of these shortsighted tactics are many—time and opportunity are lost when organizations erroneously go to the outside for New Leaders. Morale declines while spurned internal candidates demonstrate problematic behavior and become vulnerable to recruitment from other companies. Externally hired New Leaders must invest significant time and energy in recreating balance in the team. And these costs are avoidable, if Hiring Managers are willing to take a more disciplined approach to talent development and acquisition.

Stanley's Story

As a Hiring Manager for a large healthcare consulting firm, I was looking to replace a failed Marketing Director with a savvy, aggressive leader to turn around our branding strategy. That's why I chose Stanley—a well-dressed, articulate man who exuded self-confidence. Though Stanley had no experience in healthcare, his success in branding set him apart. He had a sterling reputation, and had given a popular TED Talk.

Two of my team members also applied for the position. I really valued their commitment and contributions, but both would need more development, and I didn't have the time to bring them along. They were capable people, but had been around long enough that we all knew their weaknesses. I needed a proven expert who could ramp up quickly, and that was Stanley.

It was seen as quite a coup to bring Stanley into our organization. He seemed perfect.

Since Stanley was new to the healthcare industry, the company's HR Director offered to set him up with some initial onboarding support. To that Stanley said, "Are you kidding me? If you think I need someone to hold my hand, then maybe you should have picked someone else for the job."

Not the response I expected. I immediately saw red flags, but hoped we could make this work.

I was wrong. From that point, Stanley's transition took a negative turn. He refused to take advice from peers, treating them as rivals instead of as colleagues interested in mutual success. And though he ran a large segment of the organization, Stanley wouldn't travel to the other locations, never studied the business, and failed to learn key industry terminology.

The result: Stanley and his department spiraled uncontrollably into failure. Unable to operate successfully, he became even more defensive and rude. Strategic partners felt alienated by him, Stanley's team couldn't deliver, and the organization failed to gain marketplace leadership. Also, the two internal candidates I rejected for the role left the company, taking with them institutional memory and irreplaceable customer knowledge.

After 18 months Stanley left the organization in disgrace. Long before that I learned a valuable and costly lesson: don't fall for the myth of the flawless outsider. Failing to perform due diligence on all candidates (internal and external) meant I watched helplessly as the Marketing Department lost almost two years of productivity. And I don't even want to think about the unknown opportunities we missed.

So, I changed my hiring strategy. I tapped a promising internal candidate to replace Stanley—whose first objective was to rebuild the damaged operation. She took her time, received onboarding support, focused on strengthening key skills, and is thriving in the role.

Overcoming the Myth

If the myth of the flawless outsider encourages a single external pipeline approach, how can organizations ensure they are achieving the right balance between internal moves and external hires? There are two key factors: leadership perspective and talent management. With those in mind, some suggestions to gain an equilibrium are:

- **Reject a "plug and play" mentality.**
  It is a fallacy to believe that an outside hire with related experience will become effective quickly—full ramp-up typically requires six to twelve months. The challenges to alignment and achievement of full performance are manifold, and may outweigh the benefit of the experience or skill brought by the outsider.

  In addition, a company risks becoming beholden to an external hire who may be the only leader with a particular skill set. By placing greater focus on talent development, and less on its acquisition, employers can come to view <u>anyone</u> put in the role as a work in progress. And reduce the downside risk of being overly dependent on the capabilities of one leader.

- **Topple the hero from the pillar.**
  While the organization may seek a hero, they will gain the most value from leaders who bring humility and inclusive

leadership to the role. Recovering from a difficult business challenge requires the efforts of many employees, and their New Leader's job is to set direction, inspire loyalty and drive performance.

It is wise for those dubbed heroes by Hiring Managers or others to shrug off the mantle, and strive to be more of a servant leader. As stated by Robert Greenleaf in his book, *Servant Leadership*, "Ego can't sleep. It micro-manages. It disempowers. It reduces our capability. It excels in control."[4]

- **Focus on the familiar.**
  A company is most likely to hire an outsider when the organization perceives that they don't have the skills internally to fulfill role requirements. This is where a robust talent management process becomes especially important. Identifying and cultivating up-and-comers requires time and money, but it also increases effectiveness and morale. As well, it helps organizations avoid the trap of over-relying on more expensive (and perhaps less effective) external talent.

- **Develop balanced perceptions of external candidates.**
  When there is a significant internal skill gap that drives an external recruiting focus, Hiring Managers and interviewers are most likely to overlook the flaws and personality quirks of external candidates. Don't allow your sense of urgency to curtail the interpersonal due diligence necessary for making lasting hires.

  Remember that you can expect any unusual behavior you see in the interview process to become magnified when the candidate accepts the role, particularly when they are in stressful situations. Be honest with yourself about whether the organization is able (and willing) to accept the entire New Leader, and dig deeper to understand the impact these quirks could have on their effectiveness and longevity.

- **Embrace relevant facts and data.**
  Several Hiring Managers that we have worked with remarked that they've come to regret failing to use structured interviewing techniques and pre-hire assessment reports, as those hires eventually stumbled in their roles. Indeed, one study[5] showed that Hiring Managers who utilize assessment data to inform their decisions, (rather than relying solely on their own discretion), could increase the tenure of their new hires.

In his article, "The Most Successful CEOs Come From Within," Joseph L. Bower states, "Successful CEOs are inside outsiders, executives who have grown up in the company and know how it works but have developed an outsider's perspective and have a vision of what needs to change in order to take advantage of the transformed markets." Bower also posits that an outsider's lack of familiarity with the business may cause them to over-rely on cost-cutting measures, and fail to build and implement effective growth strategies.[6]

And there is evidence that companies overpay for these (often lower-performing) external hires—one study in an investment banking firm found that the initial compensation level for external hires was 18 to 20 percent higher than for internal promotions. This research also demonstrates that these higher-paid external hires under-perform their internally-promoted counterparts for at least their first two years.[7] When internal employees are aware of these inequities, externally hired leaders are at greater risk of the disruptions brought by rivalry.

How do Hiring Managers create a more balanced approach to selection, so they don't overlook the talent right in front of them?

If an internal candidate is familiar to the organization, it is more likely that they will be known for their strengths <u>and</u> weaknesses. On the other hand, when recruiting a desirable external candidate, the Hiring Manager is more likely to focus on their strengths. This supports the notion that some leaders prefer the "shiny and new" over the old and reliable, often betting on someone they know less well than their internal candidates.[8]

The Corporate Executive Board's research report, "New Executive Assimilation," notes that some companies do see positive results with external hires. However, they also state, "Most companies' attempts at hiring an external candidates have failed due to their inability to successfully assimilate these individuals into the company."[9]

Comparison of External and Internal Candidates[10]

Consider External Candidates	Consider Internal Candidates
Company is shifting strategy or trying to execute a turna-round.	The business has a strong track record of performance.
Performance and/or talent management processes are weak, or non-existent.	Use of consistent performance and talent management processes.
The internal candidate pool lacks specific skills needed to drive strategy.	The role requires significant organization or industry-specific knowledge and skills.
Leaders believe in the importance of thought diversity.	If the culture is homogeneous, and it's unlikely an outsider will thrive.
If a strong, integrative onboarding process is in place.	If onboarding is ad-hoc, or neglected.

To drive effective selection, we suggest that Hiring Managers do the following.

- First, develop a robust, feedback-rich talent-management process that truly prepares internal leaders for big roles.

- Next, use a multivariate/multi-faceted approach to selection, with rigorous and structured interviewing and assessment for all candidates—whether external or internal to the company.

- Don't interview candidates unless you are serious about them.[11]

- Sample for role readiness and work experience.[12]

- Strive to select humans over superheroes. Remember that brilliant interview skills do not equal leadership effectiveness (and may conceal flaws and a lack of experience that will ultimately lead to candidate failure).

- Work to establish realistic expectations for New Leaders so they don't fall into the heroism trap. (For example, "I'm here to change the culture.") Humans, not heroes, deliver sustainable results. And they don't have as far to fall as those perched atop inappropriate pedestals.

- Finally, do something that most companies don't: use both pre-hire assessment and interview data to get New Leaders on the right developmental paths as they enter their roles. (Instead of waiting until their development needs become obvious to all.)

To avoid succumbing to the myth of the flawless outsider, organizations need to look internally, and not just at their possible external candidates. They should also make a realistic appraisal of the condition of the organization itself. Remember that the best defense is a good offense—heading into potential issues is a much better investment than reacting to problems when they erupt. Look for symptoms of organizational imbalance, and be honest about areas that need attention. Are you recruiting for a fresh-faced person to swoop in to fix the problems? Don't expect one individual to achieve what an entire organization has historically struggled to accomplish. Before the selection process even begins, we suggest organizations take the following steps.

1. Develop internal capacity—get your talent house in order, and prepare for the future.

2. Understand the marketplace and your customers' current (and anticipated) needs.

3. Build an accurate, robust success profile for the role.

4. Emphasize feedback and transparency so employees know where they stand, and are able to focus on specific development needs.

5. Be honest about the condition of the organization by identifying operational holes, and start addressing them.

6. Invest in the people who are in the company now, helping them to develop strategies that will help others readily recognize their contributions and potential.

7. Continuously evolve and focus on driving performance and retention.

8. Culture matters—a lot. Doggedly pursue sustainable excellence.

Difficult business circumstances can understandably cause companies to look outside for talent.[13] And, on occasion, an external hire may be the leader best-suited for the role.

Thoughtful preparation and exposure to real-life business challenges will allow current leaders to be ready to assume larger roles when the need arises. The key is to challenge assumptions, be transparent about development, and disciplined about identifying and eliminating selection bias. Recognize that no one is flawless, whether from inside or outside the organization, and that "very good" may be good enough.

One of the most important questions for building the critical talent pipeline of emerging leaders is build versus buy. A necessary first step in making this determination is to really know and understand the talent already on the team by systematically capturing that information in dynamic talent profiles. The talent profiles provide visibility into skills and performance data stored on a talent management technology platform that can then be mined to populate leadership talent pools.

Understanding individual skills, competencies, strengths, and weaknesses can provide invaluable Talent Intelligence for deciding what percentage will be developed internally through mobility and leadership development programs, and what percentage of future leaders will come from outside the organization through new hires.[14]

From "Emerging Leaders: Build Versus Buy"
by Taleo Research and
Development Dimensions International

Your Keys to Overcoming the Myth of the Flawless Outsider

What the Hiring Manager can do.

🔑 Remain aware of the pitfalls described in this chapter, and focus on talent development as part of your daily leadership activities. Recognize that externally-facing challenging assignments can accelerate capability development, and mentor your team throughout those experiences.

🔑 Through your search, task yourself with being objective when considering both external and internal candidates. Evaluate internal candidates for the role based on data, particularly when they seem to lack time in position that external candidates might offer. Spend time with your HR Partner, delineating your past experiences and observations regarding each candidate—and be open to being challenged on your opinions. Recognize the value of a structured selection process, and commit to drawing its potential benefits by consistently using it. When interviewing outside candidates, be sure to focus on unearthing their skill/experience deficits as well as capabilities. Use an inclusive process to consider internal candidates, and be open to others' challenges to your possible preconceived notions.

What the New Leader can do.

- If you are an external hire, an important first step will be to develop an understanding of why an outsider was chosen over internal candidates. Use that knowledge as a means of supporting the development of your team (especially rivals for your role—whether real, or would-be), retaining a focus on their positive attributes. Look for opportunities to give them "stretch" assignments to accelerate learning, place them on special projects, and offer them up for consideration when desirable roles become open.

- Focus on listening to, and learning from, your new colleagues. Even if you have been hired from an admired competitor, your initial role is to understand your new operation completely, resist taking impulsive action, and identify and honor existing practices before sharing any best practices you may have experienced elsewhere.

What the HR Partner can do.

- Stave off commonplace over-reliance on external talent acquisition by proactively managing your talent development/succession planning process. Be sure it includes conversations about the company's strategic direction, external challenges, changes in the marketplace, and the impact of technology on leadership requirements. Use challenging assignments, job rotation, and expatriate opportunities to develop leadership hardiness the future will require.

- Bring balance to talent acquisition by structuring a competency and behavior-based selection process. Probe all candidates in-depth about their experiences deploying the most essential skills. Facilitate a debrief meeting with all interviewers, looking within-skill, instead of within candidate. This will help eliminate bias and bring more consistency to your selection process.

VI

Why Culture Matters

It is commonly acknowledged that success (or even survival) in a role depends on a New Leader's ability to understand and successfully navigate the culture they encounter. Edgar Schein, a recognized authority in the field of Organizational Culture, says, "The bottom line for leaders is that if they do not become conscious of the cultures in which they are embedded, those cultures will manage them."[1]

In our experience, an accurate understanding of the culture is one of the most important aspects of leader transition, but it comes with significant challenges:

- How is the culture described to them as they join the organization, if it has been described at all?

- Did the recruiter and/or Hiring Manager accurately depict the current culture to the New Leader, or share a vision of how they hope the culture will function someday?

- Was the New Leader placed in the role to drive culture change?

- Is the culture the same for top leaders as it is for others deeper in the organization?

- What are the discrepancies between how the culture is broadly described by its inhabitants and how its subcultures really function?

Many, if not most, New Leaders predicate their transition plan (and behavior) on their beliefs about the organizational culture.[2] If their understanding of the culture is flawed or incomplete, their onboarding may become a process fraught with struggles. This is particularly the case when the New Leader has been hired to drive culture change.

Consider the possibility that a New Leader was selected because they were seen as "fitting" a culture that has never been fully described to them, nor openly discussed post-hire. Without that implicit understanding, it is difficult for any New Leader to embark on an effective path, and stay on track, without a clear sense of direction. Accurate awareness of the culture can serve as a kind of "onboarding GPS" for New Leaders, giving them needed information for course-correction. This feedback will speed progress as they navigate the organization, relationships and their accountabilities.

There seem to be as many definitions of culture as there are people observing these transitions—and without a common understanding, it becomes impossible to provide a consistent approach to successful culture navigation and alignment.

What Is Culture?

Organizational culture has been described in a variety of ways:

- "The way we do things around here."
- "Lessons learned that are important to pass on to the next generation of employees."
- "What we do when no one is looking."

Of course, those are the descriptions of organizational culture from each individual's own unique perspective—sort of an anthropological view. Many experts on culture, including Dan Denison

(Chairman and Founding Partner, Denison Consulting), agree that some aspects of culture are visible and measurable, including behaviors and reinforcement of norms. Other parts of culture are less visible, but still discussed—such as values and attitudes. Finally, there are those implicit components of culture that are part of the organization's subconscious, and therefore rarely discussed or questioned.[3]

In *The First 90 Days*, Michael Watkins suggests that to grasp the less obvious aspects of an organizational culture one should "peer below the surface of symbols and norms," and "carefully watch the way people interact."[4]

Importantly, all aspects and levels of culture inform and impact the performance of an organization and its New Leaders. In his book *Organizational Culture and Leadership*, Edgar Schein says, "Individual and organizational performance, and the feeling that people in an organization have about that organization, cannot be understood unless one takes into account the organization's culture."[5]

Research conducted by Denison Consulting clearly demonstrates that organizational culture drives financial (and a variety of other measures of) performance. And since New Leaders are hired to deliver results, the value of "getting" the culture seems obvious.[6]

For our purposes, "culture" is defined as the <u>performance climate</u> of an organization or operation, and is measured on four key traits. These are as discussed in detail by Dan Denison, and co-authors Robert Hooijberg, Nancy Lane, and Colleen Leif, in their book *Leading Culture Change in Global Organizations – Aligning Culture and Strategy*:

- Mission: the operation's direction, and means of accomplishing it.

- Adaptability: the extent to which the operation can become aware of, and respond to, the need to learn and change.

- Involvement: how the people connect with the work and each other, and develop capabilities.

- Consistency: the ability to predictably work together to deliver agreed-upon results.[7]

Culture is also at the root of many of the paradoxes faced by those onboarding into new roles. New Leaders are hired to make changes, fix broken things, "take us to the next level," have early impact, etc., and they must act in the context of the organizational culture in order to accomplish those imperatives. The importance of organizational culture and its impact on operations was highlighted by a respected thought leader, Peter Drucker, who is often attributed with the popular phrase, "Culture eats strategy for breakfast."

In addition, not only is there a "corporate culture" that New Leaders must navigate with agility, but there is also a culture in their own operation that New Leaders have to "get," and demonstrate respect for.

Navigating the Corporate Culture

To effectively navigate the corporate culture, New Leaders must figure out both "the way we do things around here," and "the way we don't do things around here." The organization will (directly and indirectly) signal to the New Leader what they can and can't do to drive success. Leaders who take the time to observe and ask questions about the best ways to operate, and then follow that advice, are ultimately more successful.

Leaders also have diagnostic tools such as *Culture Snapshot* (see page 171) available to them, affording them an early view into the performance climate of their own operations—the culture that will ultimately make or break their results.

For those New Leaders fortunate enough to gain this understanding of their operation, they will also be able to explore root causes of high-priority issues, and tackle them in a way that is organizationally supported and relevant.

Changing specific aspects of culture can be a daunting challenge for New Leaders, and is best achieved with a well-thought-out, inclusive and rigorous approach.

Ted's Story

Before Ted arrived, our consumer products company was facing a steady decline in the marketplace. Our processes were outdated, and the future was dim. So when my boss, Stephen, introduced Ted to our team as a peer—and the new Director of National Sales—everyone was elated. Ted came from a renowned, state-of-the-art company with cutting-edge approaches to sales and marketing. We all assumed his progressive ideas would morph our company into a success equivalent of the organization he just left. Stephen was quick to hand Ted the reins, and told him to focus on streamlining sales processes while developing the culture. We all supported Ted, and wanted him to succeed.

As Ted settled in, he seemed to fit in just fine. He was a perfect balance: a nice easy-going guy with a direct and aggressive sales approach. People liked him, and things were finally moving in the right direction.

But six months after Ted arrived, everything changed. Actually, everything completely fell apart. At one of our team meetings Ted handed out copies of a report. I thumbed through the first pages thinking nothing of it. Then Ted said, "I'm glad to have the chance to speak to you today about my findings. Stephen asked me to run a 'post mortem' on a sales initiative that failed five months prior to my arrival. I think this is a good opportunity to look candidly at ways we can improve our numbers and accelerate the sales cycle."

He walked us through, page-by-page, explaining the results. "You see, we don't need to start from scratch—we can repeat several of the steps in the original plan, but if we just avoid this one major error then the rest of the strategy looks solid."

The room got very silent. The mistake that apparently "killed" the initiative was tied to a decision Stephen made. Ted seemed baffled by the pin-drop atmosphere, asking, "Does anyone have questions?"

Stephen sat at the head of the table with a stoic look, and finally blurted out, "I think we are done here. Let's break for lunch." With that, he stood up and left.

An hour later Ted came to my office, "Hey, can we talk?"

"Sure," I said, "close the door."

Ted sat in front of my desk, looking completely bewildered. "What happened in there? I mean I did everything Stephen asked me to do. But I could tell right away that he was not happy with my report. I didn't expect that. It wasn't personal at all. It was just data we needed in order to understand how to avoid the same mistakes."

I told him, "Ted, I could tell you were not trying to put Stephen in a bad light, but that really doesn't matter. You called his mistake out in front of his staff. And didn't discuss it with him beforehand. To be honest, his reaction did not surprise me. Listen, I've been here 10 years, and when there are mistakes made here we don't focus on why or who, or even how to recover. We just move along."

Ted, who was starting to look more upset, replied, "I am really confused. At my former company everyone valued errors as learning opportunities, and we addressed them with fearless transparency. Even upper management remained open to critique, just as long as that information was used to make improvements. And I was told during the recruitment process that they wanted me to bring that approach to our own environment."

I responded, "Well, sorry to tell you this, but I can never see our company working like that. It's a different world here. You should have bounced this report off me before presenting, or at least shown this to Stephen privately before the meeting."

The next week Ted's role was reduced, and he moved from his office "with a view" into an unoccupied cubicle on a near-empty floor in our office building. He was literally— and figuratively—cast out into career oblivion. Stephen never mentioned Ted, and no one asked about him either. Ted managed to survive here for another 18 months working on special projects until he left the company to "pursue other opportunities."

I really liked working with Ted, but I think he was doomed from the start. First of all, everyone placed Ted on a pedestal, and expected that he could figure this all out on his own. Secondly, we failed Ted by not educating him about our ways. Also, we assumed that one person (someone we inadvertently labeled a "hero") could change our culture singlehandedly.

But, on the other hand, Ted contributed to his own failure by taking actions that our culture just does not allow. He could have taken some time to learn about how we really do things here. I would have been happy to fill him in, but he never asked for my advice. I think the saddest part is that Ted couldn't see (until it was too late) he was trapped in an impossible role that left him doomed from the start.

"Getting" the Operational Culture

In order to decode the culture of the operations they lead, New Leaders must step back during their first months on the job and focus on learning before trying to drive results. The paradox of transition can be felt full-force here, as New Leaders are often determined (and expected) to shake things up, and make an immediate impact. Doing so without understanding the operational terrain can cause misjudgments and missteps that may ultimately lead to the New Leader's undoing.

In addition, organizations could unknowingly neglect their role in supporting the New Leader's quest for cultural understanding. In the book *Leadership Passages*, David Dotlich, James Noel, and Norman Walker maintain that organizations make assumptions on a leader's ability to adapt, stating, "Because this senior leader has been so successful elsewhere, he'll pick things up quickly and need little hand-holding before he starts delivering on his promise."[8]

New Leaders sometimes mistakenly take premature, uninformed action because they assume that "since people downstream report to me, they will follow my direction," or, "my boss hired me to change things, and the clock is ticking." They then move forward in a manner that others may not support, and ultimately run counter to their operation's culture.[9] The consequences of this approach can range from others withholding information and efforts, to frustration and cultural "organ rejection." On the other hand, New Leaders who work closely with their Hiring Managers and teams construct deliverables that:

- Facilitate learning about the corporate and operational culture.

- Demonstrate that they have incorporated that knowledge in their decision making and action.

- Start moving the New Leader's operation toward desired goals, and performance levels, that will ultimately be more successful in both the short- and long-term.

> When new managers come into an organization, some have a need to tell everyone how good the organization they came from really was and how their mission in life is to fix all the wrongs of the new organization. When it comes to leading innovation and change, this strategy has a high chance of backfiring. When managers put down their new team, team members ask themselves two questions: "If your old company was so good, why did you leave?" And, "If it was so great, why don't you go back?"[10]
>
> Peter Stark

Changing the Operational Culture

It is understandable that organizations want to change their culture. John Kotter and James Heskett, authors of *Corporate Culture and Performance*, suggest, "Culture can have a significant impact on a firm's long-term economic performance." Most organizations are interested in improving their outcomes, so culture change would seem to be a logical next step. Importantly, the authors also note that attempts at broad organizational culture change by New Leaders (or anyone else, for that matter) can be risky, protracted, and unlikely to succeed.[11]

The odds improve when the New Leader is tasked with evolving the culture of the operation they lead (because they may have the authority, legitimacy, and budget required to drive change). Even so, leading operational culture change can be a daunting task. To be successful, a New Leader should:

- Objectively assess/measure the culture, to identify the operation's starting point and gain an outside-in perspective.

- Evaluate the constraints the existing culture creates for desired performance.

- Establish legitimacy to gain credibility. Hiring Manager and team support, along with broad communication about the compelling business case for a cultural evolution, will greatly enhance the New Leader's power to drive change.

- Include a wide variety of stakeholders in the process, drawn from all levels of the operation—and this should start during the assessment phase. As the change initiative moves forward, the New Leader's role is truly one of orchestration of commitment, effort and resources.

- Eliminate the word "change" from their vocabulary. In general, change is a word that evokes anxiety, and can cause people to feel like their previous work is being devalued. One best practice is the substitution of the phrase "what's next," implying a natural sequence of a journey, rather than a completely new direction.

Rather than ask New Leaders to drive culture change, perhaps a more effective approach would be to empower each New Leader and their team to "stretch" the culture towards their ultimate desired end-state (recognizing it as a long-term task that requires ongoing organizational support). Working with (and within) the operational culture that existed before each New Leader comes on board will help smooth their transitions, balance the paradoxical nature of onboarding, and deliver results. Operating with realistic expectations will help everyone who supports the New Leader's success thrive individually, and as a team.

The Importance of Data in Understanding Culture

A New Leader was hired to lead a troubled technology R&D function. Because the organization was in a turnaround situation that mandated change, the Leader needed rapid access to ˚data to comprehensively understand the operation, make the right decisions, and secure support for his team's new direction.

What the New Leader Already "Knew" before Accepting the Role
- The company once had a reputation as being the industry leader in scientific research, but recently experienced several product-launch flops and quality problems.
- The broader organization was "under siege," with declining market share and poor performance.
- The R&D function had a reputation for being too internally-focused and unconcerned about getting products to market as quickly as competitors.
- The executive team gave R&D six to twelve months to turn their department around.

What the New Leader Discovered on His Own
- The Hiring Manager took a hands-off approach once the Leader was placed, offering little guidance or support.
- Team engagement and morale were lower than he anticipated.
- Resources were misaligned with expected deliverables.
- The organization treated all projects equally, rather than critically evaluating their potential strategic value and attaching a priority level.
- Although the team and New Leader made strides in raising morale together, their lack of focus on external relationships and communication precluded others from recognizing the positive changes.

What the New Leader Learned through a Culture Assessment
- Various stakeholder groups had divergent expectations of the R&D team—sometimes in direct opposition to each other.
- The operation's strategy and execution plans were poorly defined and only partially implemented.

- It was very difficult to coordinate and integrate the team's work with that of other functions.
- The R&D team was expected to perform outside their scope, capabilities, and resource base. To succeed going forward, their abilities had to be viewed realistically within the context of the current climate (and its complexity).
- Skill gaps on the team needed to be addressed in real-time, as they didn't have the luxury of bringing in new talent.
- The root causes of operational ineffectiveness were uncovered and further explored.

What the New Leader (and Team) Accomplished
- R&D targeted their most pressing concerns, and root-cause understanding allowed them to directly tackle these issues.
- Strategy was considered, and the greatest points of leverage were identified. This included offloading dead-end projects and refocusing team members to get them back on track on high-value projects.
- They capitalized on their unique talents, and adopted a robust project-management methodology to trim product-development cycle time by 40 percent.
- Paid special attention to aligning and right-sizing the expectations of various stakeholders, maintaining a regular cadence of communication.
- Within six months the New Leader and team were at full performance—delivering the right projects on time and on budget.

*Data supplied by *Culture Snapshot*. For more on *Snapshot* see page 171.

Your Keys to Navigating the Organizational Culture

What the Hiring Manager can do.

    ❧ Be very clear with your final candidates about the nature of the company culture, as well as their operation. Best practice would be to perform an operational assessment such as the *Culture Snapshot* (see page 171) pre-hire, so the top candidates have a nuanced understanding of the strengths of, and challenges faced by, their new operation. This realistic job preview may scare away a candidate or two, but your eventual hire will have the advantage of an objective understanding of their operation, and will be more likely to stay committed to the role.

🟊 Guard against publicly dubbing your new hire as a culture change agent. If you wish to see improvements in operational functioning and performance, their first two to three months in the role should include a thorough, inclusive assessment of the operation, identification of the positive and negative performance impacts of the operation's culture, and a solid action plan that tackles specific ways of working.

What the New Leader can do.

🟊 Listen very carefully during the recruitment and selection process for clues about the company and operational culture, and for anyone who says that this role will include the responsibility to change the culture. This is the time to renegotiate the role and expectations with the Hiring Manager. If you fail to do so, your job could essentially become the sum total of the unrealistic expectations held by your key stakeholders.

🟊 If it becomes clear that the role requires leadership of culture change, start with an inclusive and comprehensive assessment of its current state, develop a plan you see as attainable, and work to adjust others' unrealistic expectations throughout the process.

What the HR Partner can do.

🟊 Since HR generally has a significant role in the selection of New Leaders, they have a great opportunity to provide the candidate accurate insight into both the broad corporate culture, as well as the unique culture of their operation. Resist the temptation to "pretty up" the descriptions shared with the candidates. New Leaders are better-positioned for success when they fully comprehend "the good, the bad, and the ugly" about the culture they are entering. Those who are given inaccurate descriptions of the culture may poorly navigate the culture, or feel resentful at being deceived (whether intentionally or not), which may ultimately contribute to an early departure or derailment.

‡ Be a thought partner and sounding board as the New Leader moves into the role, guiding them to a more nuanced understanding of their new world. Though it may be tempting to interpret the culture for them, it's most effective to guide the New Leader's learning process by asking thought-provoking questions and fully listening to their responses. There will be times when more direct communication about the culture is required, such as when the New Leader violates an important norm. Simply let those be the exceptions, rather than the rule.

VII

The Credibility Paradox

Popular onboarding literature urges New Leaders to make their mark quickly, with impact—gaining credibility by generating immediate results. On the face of it, this approach resonates with many in the process of onboarding into new roles. They want their employer to see them as an asset, and they are eager to demonstrate their value. However, this focus on high-impact behavior and early wins creates a paradoxical bind.

The crux of the paradox lies in the statement by James Kouzes and Barry Posner, authors of *Credibility: How Leaders Gain and Lose It, Why People Demand It*, who say, "Credibility is the foundation of leadership. This is the inescapable conclusion we have come to after more than thirty years of research into the dynamics of the relationship between leaders and constituents. People have to believe in their leaders before they will willingly follow them."[1]

This type of credibility has to be earned over time, through consistent words and work. It cannot be gained quickly. If New Leaders take a narrow approach to "proving themselves" through accomplishments and outcomes, it is often at the expense of their own long-term effectiveness. They risk alienating others and making mistakes by taking action without fully understanding potential implications.[2] Then again, if they are overly cautious or wait too long to take action, they risk being seen as unproductive or irrelevant. In other words, it's important that they get it "just right."

The process of getting it just right is one kind of establishing and maintaining dynamic equilibrium that requires New Leaders to remain aware of their surroundings and needs of their colleagues. Unfortunately, there is no simple "unlock" for building credibility. Importantly, though, a New Leader is significantly more likely to be successful when they redefine for themselves what credibility is, and what it requires. They will only be respected and valued once they have demonstrated that they respect and value their new organization and its inhabitants. If they focus too much on themselves, and not enough on learning and adapting, they are short-circuiting their own onboarding process.

New Leaders do need to deliver outcomes, but it must be the right deliverables at the right time, and in the right ways. To be credible, they must first demonstrate understanding. It is not about what they know, but how they learn, and then translate those learnings into effective actions that will build the credibility they seek. It is not about coming in with the right answers, but first asking the right questions.

Marian's Story

As the Vice President of HR at a major specialty retailer, I've certainly dealt with many challenges. Two years ago I faced probably the largest test of my 20-year career: finding a leader to fix our struggling Finance Department, and restore its reputation within the organization. Our Finance team experienced several years of weak leadership, and could no longer meet even basic performance expectations. Several of our regions actually started outsourcing their routine finance and payroll work.

Desperate for solutions, I recommended we recruit Marian as the Finance Director since she has a history of success in leading Finance operations. When she accepted the offer I met with her to go over some important details.

I said, "We're all excited you're here, Marian, and as I mentioned in our final round of interviews the Finance Department is facing some big issues. The top areas you should focus on include establishing consistent processes, rebuilding the team's capability, and mending broken trust with the other departments."

Marian said in response, "Since the Finance Department's reputation seems to be in jeopardy I should, as their leader, begin by building up my credibility within the organization."

Things went really well at the start, and I received some great feedback about Marian. Everyone who met her agreed that she was extremely likable, positive, intelligent, and her skillset was clearly what the organization needed. However, I also heard some comments that had me worried. Some shared with me that Marian didn't seem to have the same level of professionalism as the other Directors—that her appearance and approach were too casual. Though her peers and team members seemed to enjoy working with her, few took her seriously.

I met with Marian to share the feedback I was getting about her performance, and offered her the use of one of our onboarding coaches. Thankfully Marian agreed to my idea, and after a series of consultations she adapted her work style and presence to match the formality of the company.

It really was a small adjustment, but people took notice. From there, Marian developed relationships across the organization, listened actively to concerns (and responded), managed expectations, rebuilt her team, and delivered on promises while demonstrating respect for her colleagues and the culture.

As a result, Marian reestablished the department's credibility, and internal customers viewed her as a valuable partner. Eventually, the organization promoted Marian to a SVP role, and five years later she was recruited as a CFO for a large, admired global organization.

Avoid Aggression for Aggression's Sake

In most organizations, New Leaders put their reputation at risk when they barrel through challenges and discard processes. In doing so, they fail to learn from the past, ignore signals from concerned colleagues, may not gain needed support for their initiatives, and generally alienate important others.

This aggressive approach makes it challenging to include others to drive performance. Behaving in a way that damages relationships and alienates others disrupts a New Leader's momentum. If left feeling estranged, people in the organization can sidestep and even stonewall initiatives important to the New Leader. Eventually, a New Leader will use up their "new kid on the block" capital, and their reputation will be locked in place—for better or worse.

Interestingly, these New Leaders are often puzzled when confronted with the negative implications of their behavior. Because they have a blind spot, they may feel like other people who share concerns are being difficult or sabotaging their transition. With that assumption in place, New Leaders can get caught in a self-defeating cycle—repeating damaging behaviors they think are appropriate (or expected). In reality, their actions not only undermine their already fragile reputation, but also threaten developing relationships, and ultimately effectiveness. Key to their success will be the ability to step out of their own shoes and understand the impact they are having on others—and course-correct, as needed.

The Past is Not Always Prologue

Leaders are often recruited from admired organizations and hired based on notable success in their previous positions. When they assume they can achieve the same kind of results at their new employers by mirroring actions taken in their former roles, New Leaders frequently fail, and their credibility diminishes. Michael Watkins, author of *The First 90 Days*, says that some New Leaders don't "realize that what works well in one organizational culture may fail miserably in another."[3]

New Leaders may intend to reassure colleagues that they are capable and experienced by frequently mentioning prior accomplishments and employers. Unfortunately, they inadvertently come across as devaluing the organization, as well as its history, protocols, and people.

It's a matter of fact: to thrive in a role, New Leaders must take time to adapt their approach to the organization and consider its context. Unfortunately, those involved in the selection process often forget to emphasize the need for such acclimation, and New Leaders are left with the mistaken assumption that since they were selected for the role, they already are a good "fit." What they fail to realize is the fluidity of "fit" (which is really organizational relevance), and that it must be evolved over time.

Why Early Wins Can Contribute to Later Losses

New Leaders are often urged to target a few "quick hits" that demonstrate their ability to drive change and improve results. It's suggested that they pursue obvious inefficiencies, and quickly wrestle them into submission. If only it were that easy.

Pointing out the potential for onboarding risks, Mark Van Buren and Todd Safferstone state, "Knowing that they must rack up quick wins to prove themselves, new leaders often trip up during the quest for early results. In some cases, they manage to get the outcome they were seeking in a narrow sense, but the process isn't pretty, the fallout is toxic, and their ability to lead is compromised."[4]

These "low hanging fruit" are typically areas that others have already recognized as suboptimal or ineffective. Before taking on these obvious problems, a New Leader may be well-served to first understand a few important facts:

- Have there been previous attempts to solve the problem?
  - If so, what solution was attempted, and with what results?
  - If not, why hasn't the issue been tackled before now?

- Who are the people that may have either created, contributed to, exacerbated, or failed to solve the problem?

- Might it not be as straightforward as it seems, but perhaps a symptom of a more pervasive organizational issue?

- What may be the value of choosing to wait until more thorough due diligence is afforded?

In our work, we offer an alternative definition for "early wins." That the first 60 to 90 days be spent gathering data and forming impressions. At that point the New Leader meets with the Hiring Manager to share findings and recommendations. Those opinions are the true work product—the early wins—and the foundation for meaningful actions.

The New Leader who recognizes the risks in "quick hits" is typically better able to step back and evaluate the broader picture, and wait for organizational signals that the timing is appropriate for tackling the problem. New Leaders can synthesize and mirror back their early assessment, but acknowledge it is too premature to take action (and there is more to be done in understanding context and gaining support).

Transforming Tasks into Trust

New Leaders who research the history and style of their organizations, and actively seek out input from all involved, will likely find the backing they need to complete objectives in a manner that everyone supports. Importantly, they will be seen as considerate and approachable, building the relationships that are needed to reach goals effectively and sustainably.

New Leaders engender trust when they direct attention away from themselves, defer to the expertise and experience of their new colleagues, and share recognition. Van Buren and Safferstone note that leaders who share credit for achievements establish trust through that simple act, making their credibility more substantial— what they call "collective quick wins."[5] While some New Leaders think they need to build credibility by demonstrating their own contribution to the exclusion of others, the risks associated with that approach may outweigh the potential rewards. In teams, trust is foundational to collaboration and effectiveness, and teams that can't create trust cannot perform sustainably.

So Then, What is the "Right Way" to Learn About the Organization?

To establish credibility, should New Leaders completely dismantle their past practices and "start from scratch" because they are new to the organization? Not necessarily. Those looking to rapidly gain knowledge about their new operation can thoughtfully (and occasionally) share past experiences in a way that will contribute to positive outcomes. To find that balance, New Leaders should consider these questions:

1. Who are the key stakeholders to your success? How can you establish relationships and partnerships with them? Do your colleagues agree on the direction and priority of initiatives and activities?

2. Who are the most influential leaders?

3. Who might be unhappy about your appointment to this role?

4. What hidden pitfalls and barriers might keep your team from reaching their goals?

5. How do things get done here?

6. What behavior is valued? What can get New Leaders in trouble?

7. For specific initiatives ask, what is the history of the collaboration between our work areas? How does this contribute to success or failure in those situations? And what feedback do they hear about your team, overall?

The knowledge gleaned from these activities helps the New Leader establish clear and appropriate boundaries around their roles (and others' expectations). Boundary management and collaboration should be goals of organizational learning efforts for upper-level hires. Ram Charan, Stephen Drotter, and James Noel discuss both of these concepts, stating, "Managing boundaries is a matter of not just values but also specific workflow management skills. This means monitoring the flow of work between the manager of manager's unit and others in the organization, asking questions, and recommending improvements. . . . Effective cross-unit collaborations usually accelerate work processes, and a strong manager of managers can help her organization gain this competitive advantage."[6]

New Leaders who push too hard (and too quickly) to make an individual, indelible mark on an organization risk irrelevance and derailment. Conversely, effective New Leaders understand and address the paradox of gaining credibility. They balance the need to demonstrate their worth with learning about and valuing the organization, and proceed in a collaborative way that builds their reputation.

Your Keys to Establishing New Leader Credibility

What the Hiring Manager can do.

- Communicate what you expect from the New Leader, encouraging them to build a strong foundation of knowledge and relationships before "flexing their muscles" on organizational problems.

- Set (and maintain) realistic expectations among stakeholders by avoiding putting the New Leader on a pedestal. It will decrease resentment, and increase the likelihood of New Leader acceptance and support.

What the New Leader can do.

- Set aside the books on leadership transition, and place the focus on those around you rather than yourself. Helping others understand your decency and fairness will go a long way towards building your organizational credibility.

❧ Eliminate the word "change" from your vocabulary, instead communicate that your job is to lead your people on the next leg of the journey—a journey that you encourage them to join in on. Be patient—you will have the opportunity to help them drive needed change when the timing is right.

What the HR Partner can do.

❧ Use the selection process to identify New Leader strengths and weaknesses, and help them understand that their onboarding should include a focus on skill building. While organizations often herald the arrival of heroic New Leaders, it's important to right-size their self-perceptions and demonstrate humility.

❧ Observe the New Leader's transition and provide feedback about how effectively they are building their credibility. Suggest a few things they can do to demonstrate humility and listening, and direct their attention to the stakeholders groups most in need of their changed behavior.

VIII

The Importance of People
Don't Forget to Add Relationships to a New Leader's "To Do" List

New Leaders (understandably) feel pressure to perform almost immediately upon starting their new roles. They frame up their 90-day plans, identify "low-hanging fruit," and set about the work of doing their new job. A New Leader's desire to both be seen as decisive and solve problems can result in an overly task-related focus.[1] Unfortunately, what they often overlook is the positive impact that building relationships early in their tenure will have on their long-term success.[2] In over 20 years of leader onboarding work, we have found that New Leader success comes down to a very simple equation:

Relationships x (Knowledge + Feedback) = New Leader Success

With effective relationships, New Leaders can acquire knowledge and gain feedback that will help them course-correct or accelerate their transition (see graphic on the next page). Without solid relationships, New Leaders struggle. (Notice that relationships come first in the equation and have a multiplier effect. As in math equations, when you multiply something times zero, the outcome is zero. No relationships = no success.) And the higher they go in the organization, the greater the impact of relationships on performance. Leaders who think that their senior leadership role brings inherent power that precludes the need for relationship development are at risk of failing in their role. According to one study, up to 60 percent of derailed leaders attribute their failure to their lack of focus on forging effective working relationships.[3]

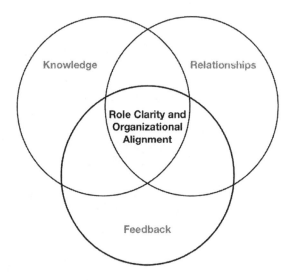

The New Leader who doesn't have a nuanced understanding of the importance of relationships can be thwarted on every front. Regardless of the substance of their job description and formal duties, New Leaders can't force followers or demand support. For their priorities to be accomplished, others need to adopt shared goals and see them as important. Without that partnership, New Leaders often fumble and stumble through their first several months on the job. The clumsiness of their transition only serves to alienate others and further deprive New Leaders of needed knowledge and feedback. For those New Leaders who wish to enjoy longer-term tenure and success, the commitment to building relationships will have a return on investment that greatly exceeds the effort required.

While organizations largely believe the task of relationships lies with the New Leader, it is recommended that they be provided support to structure their transition. In the following pages we list six relationship rules that organizations and New Leaders should consider.

CFOs who report being satisfied with their performance in the first hundred days are far more likely than those who are not satisfied to report having held in-person meetings with both the core finance team and the broader finance staff.[4]

"The CFO's First Hundred Days: A McKinsey Global Survey"
McKinsey Quarterly (December, 2007)

Rule #1: Don't Just Set out to Meet People

Many organizations encourage their New Leaders to follow a "meet-and-greet" calendar that familiarizes them with colleagues across the business. This can be helpful, but must be handled in a way that truly adds value for all involved. For success you must move beyond the "meet and greet" to a deeper, more meaningful conversation—<u>about them</u>. Don't worry about trying to make yourself understood—instead, seek to understand the needs of your key stakeholders. Get their perspective on your operation and the extent to which it is delivering to their expectations. Ask for feedback about what your team can do to be more effective.

Importantly, see these first conversations as the beginning of ongoing dialogue and relationships. Don't just do a "drive-by" by holding only an initial meeting—keep momentum building by appropriately seeking them out and deepening relationships. Your administrative support can be invaluable here—define a cadence of regular meetings that will help your important stakeholders understand your commitment to these relationships. By giving them this interpersonal due process, you are learning about them while simultaneously signaling your respect and desire to become a valued partner.

Rule #2: At the Beginning, the Only Thing That Matters Is Where <u>They</u> Have Been

Even if you were hired to fix major problems, be careful to look to the past before thinking (or communicating) about yourself, or the future. Marshal Goldsmith and Mark Reiter urge New Leaders to listen. "To learn from people, you have to listen to them with respect. Again, not as easy to do as you might imagine. It too requires the use of unfamiliar muscles."[5] And New Leaders in a hurry or under pressure are prone to overlooking the value of this advice. A rich history exists in and around your operation, and you can learn valuable lessons about your team from it by asking:

- What do they see as their own strengths?

- Which problems do they wish they could fix?

- What are their hypotheses about the true root cause of the problems?

- What are some things they have already tried?

- What worked and didn't work, and why?

Importantly, once your team and colleagues feel understood, you will then be allowed to help them move forward, particularly if you don't judge or devalue where they have been. Instead of being critical, consider an alternative way of thinking: the world around us is demanding that we continue to evolve, and we need to identify what we are required to do in order to be successful in the future. Taking a "no harm, no foul" approach to your focus on operational effectiveness will support learning and decrease others' anxieties about you and your transition.

Rule #3: The Only Bad Feedback Is <u>No</u> Feedback

We all understand the importance of first impressions—the distinction in successful onboarding is that we don't try to dazzle people with our brilliance, but instead work to demonstrate how much we value them.

By building effective relationships, we create a conduit for feedback—both direct and indirect. Valued partners will:

- Define what "success mode" looks like by sharing the "dos and don'ts" of the corporate culture.

- Provide advice about navigating other relationships and meeting expectations—both individual and collective.

- Give you a view into how your operation is perceived. It's essential to have an external perspective on your team's strengths and weaknesses, their history, and the expectations held for them by others.

- Share their real-time observations about your transition privately, respectfully, and while there is still time to course-correct, (if needed).

It is a bonus if you have access to something like *LevelSet: Early Feedback* (see page 171), where you can gain insight into your own effectiveness as a leader in transition. If that is not available to you, keep seeking information until you are reasonably certain of your understanding. Without feedback, you will be driving blind.

Rule #4: Some People Are More Important to You Than Others

You have been hired to implement strategy, and good strategy recognizes that we must place greater weight on certain goals and initiatives to truly drive success. Similarly, it is possible to have positive relationships with all key stakeholders while placing stronger emphasis on relationships with certain people. To invest your time and energy most wisely:

- Identify your top priorities.

- Create a stakeholder analysis that considers those priorities, as well as the needs and expectations of those most important to you and your operation (or most greatly impacted by it).

- Understand where you may need support or have the greatest possibility of gaining it.

- Assign priority levels to stakeholders.

- Consider how they may view you and your operation.

- Recognize how your relationship-building approach may impact others.

- Make the largest investments of time and attention where it best serves your goals, remembering that those who are unhappy with you and your operation may need the most from you, at least in the short-term.

- Then keep coming back to all of your stakeholders with varying frequency and involvement, depending on what you need to accomplish (and what they need from you). Importantly, make your interactions about their success and how you can support it.

Ram Charan, Stephen Drotter, and James Noel note the need for balance in *The Leadership Pipeline*: "In some companies, relationship-building has political overtones, suggesting brown-nosing and other manipulative behaviors. In these instances, it takes a concerted effort by managers and strong coaching by their boss to overcome this hurdle."[6] Remember that balancing your priorities with those of important others is important. And those who want more time and energy from you than you see as appropriate are likely to be unhappy about your priorities, and that your actions may signal a departure from how your predecessor interacted with them. They may react to their unhappiness by escalating issues without first consulting you, challenging you in meetings, or failing to pass along information that you need. It may be helpful to see them not as "difficult," but as people who must adjust to a new way of interacting with your area—and who have concerns about whether they will get what they need. A focus on supporting their success will be time well-invested.

Key Stakeholder Relationships

	Insights They Offer	Questions to Ask
Hiring Manager	Access to, and insights about, higher-level leaders, the formulation of organizational strategy, and overall expectations.	• How should I engage with your peers? • What can you share with me about the organization's management structure?
Direct or Skip-Level Reports	Winning over the team should be a priority to fairly and accurately size up skills, establish order, and defuse negative emotions and/or potential rivalries.	• How have we collectively handled previous management changes? • How can I help you adapt to my transition as your leader?
Peers	Organizational assessment, and feedback about team performance from the other departments.	• What does your department need from me and from my team? • How does my team rate in meeting those needs?
Customers & Suppliers	Opportunity to gain a broader perspective, establish shared goals,[7] and become skilled in the give-and-take of negotiation.	• What weaknesses have you encountered in our products or operation? • What is the primary goal of your relationship with our organization?

Rule #5: You Never Know When You're Meeting a Person or a Process

In many organizations, the people around us hold the keys to our success because they understand how to get things done. The larger, or older, the company, the more likely that process workarounds are the norm. While there may be a formal process on the books, it's important to learn how things really get done. It is wise to respect a process, but it is equally helpful to discern whether the process in place is formal or informal, and if there's something extra you must do to get things accomplished. The "who" of a process is also crucial—if you can identify those who understand and navigate well, things will be much easier.

If you take on process design/redesign as a priority in your new role, remember that those who are used to (formally or informally) regulating some process or workflow will likely want to continue to do so. Rather than labeling them as "change resistant," see them as people who remain committed to driving outcomes, and work to increase their investment in the new way of doing things. Include them in the body of work that creates or redesigns processes. And be sure that this changed order of things leaves them with the tools necessary to drive the results for which they are accountable.

Rule #6: Sometimes the Most Important Relationships Are the Ones That Create Discomfort

As you enter your role, expect to encounter some unpleasant interactions, often with people who are unhappy with you or your operation. As a New Leader, ignoring problems won't make them go away, but facing into them ineffectively can worsen the situation. At least two kinds of colleagues may warrant a deeper investment of your time and attention before serious conflict arises: unhappy internal customers who depend upon your area for their success, and various rivals for your role. Remember that, in both cases, a very basic equation applies:

They Wanted Something + Didn't Get What They Wanted = Anger

Because your new colleagues generally want positive relationships with newcomers, some will resist your initial invitation to share the whole history of the operation's relationship with them. Another barrier to transparency may be that the direct communication of negative emotions goes against their cultural norms. Your effectiveness will depend on your ability to recognize the subtle clues your internal customers offer you—sometimes in the form of extended silence when asked a question, or a quick change of topic.

To win them over, and get a better sense of what's real, pay close attention to what they say (and <u>don't</u> say).

Be sure to give your relationship time to mature before tackling tough issues. Resist the temptation to go right to the heart of the problem in your first conversation. Pace yourself and look for opportunities as time passes. It may help to determine whether true role clarity exists between your areas—role conflict is often at the heart of workplace strife. If you develop significant concerns, broaden your focus to gain others' perspectives and proceed from there.

You will run into at least one team member or colleague who wished to be chosen for the role you now occupy. And these rivals may fall into one of several camps: actual candidates in the selection process (who didn't get the role), those who wanted the prestige of the role but may not meet all hiring criteria, and perhaps most problematically, those who would never be considered for a promotion to this role. People from all three camps will likely have some discomfort with you, but may require different leadership behavior.

While it would be ideal for New Leaders to experience positive relationships with all key stakeholders, it is also an unrealistic expectation. However, investing in understanding and improving difficult relationships will likely lead to better outcomes.

New Leaders who recognize that relationships will make or break their transitions take an important first step in successfully occupying their new role. Indeed, managing relationships will be important to New Leaders every day they remain in the role, for both the short- and long-term. Using some of the methods outlined above, will greatly enhance the chances of lasting success.

Your Keys to Building and Sustaining New Leader Relationships

What the Hiring Manager can do.

   ♦ Provide your new hire with insights into individuals on their key stakeholder list (that you helped them generate). Make it as factual as possible, and allow the New Leader to form their own opinions.

- **↟** Make sure that the New Leader has identified and planned for the relationships that they need to succeed. Go through the key stakeholder list with the New Leader, and agree on a strategy for developing relationships with your peers. Take the time to define appropriate boundaries for those peer interactions. Don't be a command-and-control gatekeeper—be courageous enough to allow the New Leader to develop those relationships independently. They will know they have been successful when they feel they can discuss important issues without including you (unless your input is needed).

What the New Leader can do.

- **↟** Do a thorough key stakeholder analysis and relationship plan, using information and strategies developed to help you track the evolution of your interactions. Your Hiring Manager and HR Partner can assist you with some of the finer details. Find out what these stakeholders care most about, what they need from you and your operation, and gather insights into their operations and priorities. Capture this information on an ongoing basis, and build upon your existing knowledge base. Construct a comprehensive approach to deepening relationships with each individual listed.

- **↟** Work to create and develop strong relationships with your colleagues so they feel comfortable in providing you feedback. And when they do bring you any constructive (or seemingly negative) feedback, see this as a positive sign that you have built the rapport required for success.

What the HR Partner can do.

- **↟** Prep the New Leader for the "meet-and-greet" process, and debrief as it draws to a close. Review the New Leader's key stakeholder analysis, and work to highlight any potential issues. Provide insight for next steps in deepening and strengthening relationships.

❗ While others may seek your thoughts about, or share their opinion of, the New Leader, be detached and professional while hearing them out. Advise only where appropriate, and be cautious about being seen as going on record about the New Leader. Encourage them to share real-time feedback with the New Leader where possible, then take any remaining concerns directly to the New Leader.

IX

Rivals
They Go with the Territory

Whether a New Leader is being brought in from the outside, or elevated into a higher role, there's a good chance they will work with someone who wanted their job. There may be people in the organization who were interviewed, had been asked to interview and opted not to, or were not asked to at all. And those would-be rivals likely think they're more qualified for the role than the New Leader—or may at least resent them for being there. This belief may not be based on logic, and it's crucial to be aware of the role it plays in the hidden dynamics of rivalry. New Leaders need to understand what has happened in the selection process, and how possible rivals feel about it, so that they can build effective working partnerships.

Rivals are important to New Leader success in many ways—and they are not "the enemy," even if they may sometimes behave like one. Rivals understand the culture, other leaders, and "where the bodies are buried." They have key historical, functional, and technical knowledge. Failure to bring rivals into the fold means New Leaders lack needed information. This knowledge gap can result in missteps and missed opportunities, as well as incomplete or fragmented team formation. Strained relationships increase misunderstanding and misattribution of motive, and block essential communication. If a rival played an interim role in the New Leader's position during the search for a permanent leader, the challenges faced may be compounded.

The Costs of Rivalry

While some think of rivalries as a normal part of office politics, they can be corrosive. Some costs include:

- Workplace warfare—whether open or veiled—is destructive in untold ways.

- Failed initiatives and lower levels of performance.

- Derailed Leaders—if not attended to properly, rivals can unseat New Leaders.

- Undermined trust among peers or team members.

- Lack, or distortion, of communication (and insufficient knowledge transfer).

- Reduced risk-taking and innovation on initiatives.

- Lost potential for collaboration on all levels.

- Decreased team morale, engagement, and overall effectiveness.

Rivalry Redefined

When asked to identify potential rivals for Newly-placed Leaders, Hiring Managers and HR Partners frequently tell us, "There are none—no one else was qualified for this role." But with some gentle probing, they soon recognize that there may be several rivals in place. It is then that they see the need to expand their definition of rivalry to accurately assess (and manage) the risks rivals create for New Leaders.

In our work, we define a rival as "anyone who may be unhappy to have this New Leader in this role." While logic may suggest that there were no viable internal candidates for the position, it is the emotional state of the would-be rivals that must not be ignored. Left unattended, they can do untold damage to the New Leader, team, and organization.

The Consequences of Envy in the Workplace

Tanya Menon and Leigh Thompson conducted research on the emotional response of rivals in the workplace. In their article, "Envy at Work," they assert that negative consequences can be inflicted upon more than the rival's target. They state:

"Envy damages relationships, disrupts teams, and undermines organizational performance. Most of all, it harms the one who feels it. When you're obsessed with someone else's success, your self-respect suffers, and you may neglect or even sabotage your own performance and possibly your career. Envy is difficult to manage, in part because it's hard to admit that we harbor such a socially unacceptable emotion."[1]

Rivalry Has Many Faces

There are very few rivals who announce themselves to New Leaders by publicly sending "a shot across the bow." Though they may be unhappy with the presence of the New Leader, they also understand that being overtly hostile can be personally and professionally risky.

In fact, it's often not what the rival does, but what they <u>don't do</u>, that becomes problematic for New Leaders. While the phrase "passive aggressive" is overused, colleagues who choose not to support what's important to a New Leader (without admitting it) may fit into that category. And the invisibility of their contempt can increase the difficulty of recognizing the presence and threat of these potential rivals.

Rivals take many forms, but most fit into one of seven categories:

1. **The Interim Leader**

   A person who has served in the New Leader's role as a stand-in for some period of time. This often is someone who was never formally considered for the job—and may have been told so. But that didn't stop them from wanting the position, or seeing their temporary appointment as an "audition."

   Think about it—if someone was capable of "holding down the fort" during the search for a New Leader, how could the Interim Leader not harbor negative feelings about being overlooked for the permanent role?

2. **The Upstart**

   Often a younger, ambitious leader who has been dubbed a high-potential by the organization. The main issue with these leaders is how they overestimate their capabilities, and lack the wisdom that comes with experience. They might have natural leadership ability, but it takes experience and maturity (that Upstarts lack) to become properly prepared for high-level leadership roles.

   Organizations often confuse the Upstart by publically lauding their talents and ambitious mindset when they are, in fact, not yet ready for a high-level promotion.

3. **The Technical Expert**

   An individual who has a deep experience (maybe even more than the New Leader) in specialized disciplines and technologies that are valued by the organization. This rival usually surfaces in high-level technical leader transitions, such as in IT or R&D functions. Technical Experts tend to favorably compare their own technical ability with that of a New Leader, yet ignore (or significantly underestimate the importance of) the other skills required for success in the role.

   Failure to identify and address this blind spot means that New Leaders can have rivals lying in wait—from the moment their hire is announced or their bio becomes public.

4. **The Feedback-Deprived Team Member(s)**

   This person—most often found in "nice" companies—has spent most of their career cut off from needed feedback. Well-intended colleagues might hold back corrective feedback out of a desire to preserve relationships. This self-awareness void can cause Feedback-Deprived Team Members to remain out of touch with their own competency levels and impact on others.

   Since they see themselves significantly more positively than others do, and have the potential to be hurt by their exclusion from consideration for the position, Feedback-Deprived Team Members are especially vulnerable. No matter the reason, withholding feedback places this individual at a disadvantage—and it borders on disrespectful.

5. **The Culture Keeper**

   This individual understands the organizational history and holds knowledge about why the operation engages in certain practices. Many organizations respond to daunting marketplace challenges by hiring New Leaders to serve as "change agents." If change-agency (or the transition itself) is mishandled, it can naturally cast some team members in the role of Culture Keeper.

   Well-intentioned, but clumsy, change efforts cause this rival to oppose misguided New Leaders. And those same New Leaders need the Culture Keeper's support to gain credibility or become successful. If you ever hear, "That's not the way we do things around here," then you likely have a Culture Keeper in your midst.

6. **The Former Peer**

   As a now direct report, this type of rival can be one of the most difficult to manage. According to former Fortune 500 executive, Lisa Quast, "Oftentimes, former co-workers, either because of jealousy or out of habit, won't want to treat you as the boss; they may want to continue treating you as one of the group."[2]

   And though setting appropriate boundaries is a start, it wouldn't hurt to make a point of demonstrating respect for the Former Peer.

7. The Peer Rival

This rival may not be a direct report, but instead a peer who is not interested in seeing the New Leader succeed. In fact, they may actually hope for failure. As David Dotlich, James Noel, and Norman Walker assert, "Peers can be bad in confusing ways—one day they may be supportive and the next become competitive and withholding. Today's allies may suddenly turn into future competitors because of shifting organizational structures, priorities, or roles."[3]

Intentionally withholding information is the opposite of adding value. We are deleting value. Yet it has the same purpose: To gain power. It's the same old need to win, only more devious.[4]

From *What Got You Here Won't Get You There*
by Marshall Goldsmith and Mark Reiter

Charlotte's Story

When I was hired as an Executive Vice President at a leading pharmaceutical company, I was responsible for product development and testing while managing a sprawling global operation. Though all seemed to be going well, a potential rivalry was bubbling below the surface—and everyone knew it except for me.

Maxwell, a 25-year veteran of the company, was seen as a high-potential leader throughout his career here. He already held a VP role at the company, and I learned (after I arrived) that in the process of selecting a leader for my position, Maxwell was a solid candidate. However, Maxwell lacked the global leadership experience that was so important to this struggling company's turnaround. With that perspective, the hiring committee chose to bring in an outsider with proven experience. Although Maxwell was clearly told he lacked needed qualifications to be promoted into the role, it had been one he aspired to win throughout his tenure. And his ambitions were clear to all.

A short time into my role, an onboarding coach conducted individual interviews with more than 20 senior leaders on my extended team. The questions were designed to get their perspective on my progress as their leader. When I read my final feedback report I was astonished to see their responses. All but one expressed concern about Maxwell being passed over in favor of me. In these candid conversations, most shared that they felt loyal to (and protective of) Maxwell, and wondered if he was hurt by the decision. They didn't understand why he had not won the role, and many stated that they worried about a potential conflict between the two of us.

For whatever reason, prior to the interviews no one felt they could share this with me in person. It was the first time I understood the magnitude of my team's struggle around my appointment. I also realized that Maxwell likely had some issues we needed to address together.

With this in mind, I immediately approached Maxwell, and asked for his honest thoughts and feelings about the situation. I also asked for his advice on ways we could partner and encourage unity within the team.

Once we came to agreement on these important goals, we addressed the group together. We stood before the team, and I said, "It's time to finally bring an important issue to the surface and discuss it openly. Maxwell and I have been talking and working details out between the two of us, and he would like to say a few things."

To a noticeably unsettled group he spoke. "Yes, as everyone suspects, I was very disappointed to have missed the opportunity for this role. My entire career has been at this company, and I felt I was ready for this promotion."

Then, to everyone's surprise, Maxwell said this, "However, Charlotte brings a broader view of the global pharma market than I do, and she has needed turnaround experience. She can help us succeed. I support her, and hope you do too."

Maxwell's candor and openness encouraged others on the team to relax and feel confident they could discuss what many were too fearful to mention.

Back when I first received my feedback report, I have to admit I was not sure how to address this situation. But as Maxwell and I worked together, I realized that offering him a safe platform to say exactly what is on his mind, actively listening, and demonstrating that I respect his experience helped defuse a potentially volatile situation.

Seven years later I am still in the role, and our team has been able to weather a turbulent business environment. We executed a large-scale turnaround in a declining market, and have returned our company to profitability.

Bringing Rivals Back into the Fold

In order to engage in a successful transition, every New Leader must identify and address the inherent challenges associated with workplace rivalries. It's important to recognize that it may not be possible to win over every rival, but a New Leader who can coax them onto neutral ground in their relationships will have removed a significant barrier to success.

Because rivals assume various forms, defusing every type of rivalry requires slightly different approaches—and should be addressed thoughtfully. Here are some solutions a New Leader can use to bring rivals back into the fold.

Key actions to take with an Interim Leader.

- Publically demonstrate respect and appreciation for what the Interim Leader has accomplished.

- Learn from them by asking questions and truly listening.

- Balance their perspective with other things you are learning. And keep your opinions to yourself—at least for a month or two.

- Talk with the Interim Leader about their career and aspirations.

- If they aspire to hold the role you have (and you believe they hold the potential to be successful), support their development for the role or readiness for promotion to another position.

To corral the Upstart.
- First, spend time with your HR Partner to understand the company's talent management process. Learn which skills and behaviors caused this leader to be identified as a high-potential. Identify any skill gaps or overdone strengths.

- Then meet with the Upstart to learn about their past contributions and future goals. Ask about feedback they have received, investments they have made in their own growth, and discuss where gaps still exist. Direct their energy towards closing those skill gaps to show your support of their career objectives.

- Consider involving them in special projects that can foster additional development and absorb some of their excess capacity.

- Help them identify and connect with other mentors in the organization, and find ways to help increase their visibility within their current role (but never at your own expense).

- Follow up, stay connected, and provide the Upstart balanced feedback that recognizes accomplishments while encouraging them to continue building skills.

Deal successfully with the Technical Expert.
- Get grounded in the competency profiles used by your organization's talent management process. Do a self-evaluation, and be frank with yourself about your own strengths and weaknesses (especially in technical areas).

- Get feedback from key stakeholders, learn important acronyms and verbiage, and strive to increase your technical aptitude from day one.

- Help the Technical Expert evaluate their capabilities against their career goals. While a leadership role may look appealing from the outside, it might turn out that the Technical Expert isn't really interested in all it truly requires.

- Create an understanding that although a top leadership role in a technical function may require specific skills as the "price of admission," there are other kinds of strengths— such as strategy development and leadership—that are key. Reinforce that anyone who wants to advance their career needs to expand their skill set to these broader areas. (And they will develop most quickly if they get multi-rater feedback, and make a sustained effort in self-enhancement.)

- Recognize that the Technical Expert likely sees technical proficiency as being the most important aspect of your role. Find ways to acknowledge their capabilities, and be sure they are challenged enough in their current role. Where appropriate, have them represent your operation in cross-functional teams (while coaching them on how to balance their technical and non-technical/leadership skills).

To help the Feedback-Deprived Team Member(s).
- First form your own opinions about each team member— and resist the attempts of others to brief you (unless you consult about someone who is in a formal, corrective performance-management process).

- Then seek input from your HR Partner and other colleagues about the effectiveness of each team member, and remain personally detached while gathering this information.

- Ask all team members to brief you on their work and accomplishments. Encourage them to share a portfolio of their best efforts. Learn about their strengths, weaknesses, and goals. Then evaluate how your direct reports' goals line up with what you have observed and heard about their effectiveness.

- Where significant skill or behavioral gaps exist, identify the best strategy for addressing them with the Feedback-Deprived Team Member. Multi-rater feedback can be helpful, as can books like *Leadership and Self-Deception: Getting Out of the Box* (by The Arbinger Institute).

- Most importantly, deliver your observations with respect and patience. It can be embarrassing to gain feedback that has been long-withheld. But it is ultimately what's best for that team member.

To successfully interact with a Culture Keeper.
- Don't dismiss them or their comments. Rarely is a New Leader hired to singlehandedly execute a complete overhaul of an operation—they need partnership from their new colleagues. And even a turnaround requires successful navigation of the existing organizational culture. Someone who understands the barriers is a valuable asset to a New Leader.

- Recognize that Culture Keepers are communicating organizational norms to you—and this is valuable information for your success. Enlist them as key advisors in your change initiatives, and keep the lines of communication open. Focus on your own change leadership. There are some great resources, such as *Switch: How to Change Things When Change Is Hard* by Chip and Dan Heath, and *The Heart of Change: Real-Life Stories of How People Change Their Organization* by John P. Kotter and Dan S. Cohen.

- Remember that when people object to change, they are usually concerned about their own ability to continue delivering results using new processes or methods. So respect their desire to perform, and work together to find ways to preserve their ability to drive results.

- Avoid using the phrase, "When I worked at _____ company, we did _____," in your first couple of months in the role. This common mistake made by New Leaders signifies a lack of respect for the operation. Culture Keepers are often quick to react negatively to these comments, and are probably expressing opinions also held by others, in addition to their own.

- Understand the Culture Keeper's career interests. Should they truly be interested in a leadership role, design opportunities to help them move in that direction and fill in the gaps they currently have.

Shifting a Former Peer to collaboration.

- Since this person is now a direct report of yours, you have the responsibility of managing their performance. Make sure you are being supportive of their success and not visibly jockeying for position with them.

- It can be disconcerting to manage a Former Peer, and you both will experience an adjustment period. During that time, look for evidence of a desire to collaborate and reinforce it (while staying mindful of things they are doing that they shouldn't, or aren't doing that they should).

- If you have a history of competing with this direct report, be the first to model inclusion and collaboration. Ask for their involvement—and value it. For the first couple of months, share only positive opinions with this rival.

- Talk with your Former Peer about their career and aspirations, and support their development.

- If they aspire to hold the role you have (and you believe they hold the potential to be successful), support them in developing readiness for a future promotion. If their ambitions lie elsewhere, do what you can to expose them to other leaders and opportunities, as well as special projects that will expand their capabilities while increasing visibility.

Shifting a Peer Rival to collaboration.

- It's important to note that rivalrous behavior is about the New Leader only some of the time. Consider whether your work context naturally pits you against each other. Do you have a shared boss who plays favorites, or is inattentive to the team?

- Establishing a common goal with your Peer Rival is a powerful way to move things in the right direction.

- Learn as much as possible about their operation and accountabilities. Then evaluate if the roles, priorities, and processes intersect with your own.

- Ask the Peer Rival for a historical perspective, feedback about your team, transition advice, and for ways your own operation can support their success.

- If you're in a hyper-competitive culture, model collaborative behavior whenever possible, but recognize that you may be swimming upstream and in need of adjusting your own expectations.

Defusing the Landmine: Getting to (at Least) Neutral Ground

Leader transitions can be fraught with emotion (for the New Leader, as well as their colleagues). While focusing on the rational side of business is required, New Leaders who ignore the emotional impact of their appointment do so at their own peril. The behavior of the rival may not be overt, but a powerful or well-liked rival can continuously undermine the New Leader to the point of their eventual irrelevance or ineffectiveness. This unfortunate "failure to thrive" is likely to be attributed to the New Leader's shortcomings, rather than the actions (or inactions) of key others.

The common denominators in the strategies suggested above are the importance of listening, learning, communicating effectively, and collaborating when starting a new role. Doing so will help you bring rivals into the fold, and have broader, enduring benefits as well. If the approach fails to deliver desired results, it may be time to elect to take more drastic action. But that path is not to be chosen lightly, or without first having exhausted the constructive alternatives.

That Lincoln, after winning the presidency, made the unprecedented decision to incorporate his eminent rivals into his political family, the cabinet, was evidence of a profound self-confidence and a first indication of what would prove to others a most unexpected greatness. . . .

It soon became clear, however, that Abraham Lincoln would emerge the undisputed captain of this most unusual cabinet, truly a team of rivals. The powerful competitors who had originally disdained Lincoln became colleagues who helped him steer the country through its darkest days.

From *Team of Rivals: The Political Genius of Abraham Lincoln*
by Doris Kearns Goodwin[5]

Your Keys to Identifying and Engaging the New Leader's Rivals

What the Hiring Manager can do.

- If you must place an Interim Leader in role while searching for the permanent hire, be clear about whether that person is genuinely a potential candidate for the role. If so, describe the selection process accurately, and confirm that external candidates are being considered.

- If the Interim Leader is not being considered for the permanent position, be explicit about this fact (and coach them on the skills and experience that will make them promotable into the next appropriate opening).

What the New Leader can do.

❧ Talk with the Hiring Manager and HR Partner about those colleagues who either were considered as candidates for the role, or perhaps more importantly, weren't considered (but had hoped to be).

❧ Focus on their goals and aspirations for future promotions, and set on a path of developing them to be ready when the next opportunity arises. If they are considered a "high professional" and not likely to be promotable in the future, consider how their job might be enlarged or enriched to challenge them (and their skill development).

What the HR Partner can do.

❧ Appropriately advise the New Leader about all potential rivals for the role, including the skill and experience gaps that might have precluded their selection. Provide developmental resources to enhance their future performance and career growth.

❧ Observe interpersonal dynamics between the potential rivals and New Leader, providing feedback and coaching to all affected parties.

X

The Importance of Feedback: Early and Ongoing

The Window of Judgment Slams Shut for Many New Leaders

When we ask clients how long it takes before their organization informally judges whether its New Leaders "get it" or not, they usually say somewhere between 60 and 90 days in the role. Talya Bauer states, "Research and conventional wisdom both suggest that employees get about 90 days to prove themselves in a new job. . . . The faster new hires feel welcome and prepared for their jobs, the faster they will be able to successfully contribute."[1] We call this the "window of judgment," and it is a source of great concern. Think about it. This means that before official nameplates are mounted on their office doors, many New Leaders could be headed for the exit—a distressing thought for those who invest significantly in recruiting the best candidates for these roles.

Corporate partners acknowledge that the window of judgment is closing on New Leaders much sooner than it used to. Ten years ago, clients indicated that this window stayed open for a more forgiving four to six months. Since then, many factors have conspired to speed up the process of judging New Leaders (including the influence of technology, greater awareness of the importance of onboarding, as well as an economic context that creates greater anxiety/urgency among Hiring Managers and New Leaders). This shrinking timeline underscores the importance of New Leaders understanding their early impact. They need to lean into their onboarding, learning to identify and head off potential issues while there is still time for recovery.

Jason's Story

A large retailer hired me as their CIO in hopes that I could restructure and outsource some key operations. I've had experience with similar directives, so I felt rather confident going in.

During the first few months, my colleagues would often reminisce about my predecessor, Susan. They admired her because she was both trustworthy and approachable. You don't see that very often at the C-level. But then again, this organization prides itself for being known as a warm and friendly workplace. I realized that to win them over I would need to adjust my usual left-brained, formal approach by being more casual and conversational. Although it is common for IT leaders to emphasize logic and science, I genuinely cared about my colleagues and team, and hoped that over time they would see my commitment to their success.

As part of the company's onboarding program, I was given access to the *LevelSet: Early Feedback* tool. When I read through the final report with my onboarding coach, I was relieved to see that both my peers and direct reports respected my technical skills and confidence. However, other responses disclosed that some perceived me as too sharp, overly direct, and often disrespectful. As I looked more closely at their statements, I recognized I had a major communication gap to address. One theme in the report kept surfacing: it's not what I say, it's how I say it.

I didn't shy away from these comments. In fact, it seemed important to gain more insight. So I scheduled a series of one-on-one follow-up meetings with my colleagues and team members, encouraging them to be open and honest. I also found it helpful to ask my peers to signal me (real-time in meetings) if I ever used a tone or words that could be misinterpreted as rude or cold.

It turns out that having access to honest feedback (and being willing to accept it) opened the door to stronger working relationships. It also gave me insight into the culture, and I became a trusted partner and leader. As a result, my team and I were able to collectively restructure and streamline our operations—a success that we all shared.

New Leaders Often Forget to Adapt Their OnBoarding Approach

If we think about feedback in a mechanistic way, a system monitors some measure of equilibrium (for example, thermostats sense a change in temperature). When the balance is disturbed (the temperature rises), the system sends a signal to compensate for that disruption (feedback to provide more cooling). With that adjustment, things return to a stabilized state.

Now, imagine New Leaders as a part of an organizational system. While we hope they behave in ways that maintain equilibrium, New Leaders may, in fact, do just the opposite. They often lack knowledge about the organization, and interact in ways that can be viewed as disruptive. This increases the risk that they will:

- Make decisions that are inconsistent with organizational expectations, strategy, or norms (or are just downright ineffective).

- Struggle in relationships with people who are in the position to either enhance or undermine their success.

- Overestimate their own capabilities and fail to deliver on important objectives.

- Exclude valuable sources of information from their thought processes and implementation.

- Lead their teams in ways that ignore their lessons of experience, and take them down the wrong path.

In all five cases above, New Leader behavior creates a disturbance in the system. Unfortunately, clients indicate that these same New Leaders are rarely given needed feedback in a timely and transparent fashion. In fact, many acknowledge that their New Leaders might operate feedback-free until their first performance review (which could be up to a year after their start date, and nine months after the window of judgment closes). This knowledge vacuum can be devastating for organizations and their New Leaders—equilibrium and performance suffer, and New Leaders flail about.

Insufficient feedback also often serves to rob New Leaders of their dignity by assuming they would not value and accept input.[2] Experienced colleagues and direct reports already know where the New Leaders fall short, but there is no real way for the New Leader to readily self-assess. Failing to close this knowledge gap can prove to be disrespectful, embarrassing, and pointless. Employers need to assume that all New Leaders come to their roles with a strong desire to perform in ways that are acceptable to their Hiring Managers and organizations. So, if a New Leader demonstrates ineffectiveness, it could be attributed, at least in part, to a broken feedback loop in the onboarding process. Someone is depriving the New Leader of the understanding of what is going wrong, as well as potential solutions.

Why New Leaders "Fly Blind"

New Leaders operate without accurate insight into their early effectiveness for a variety of reasons:

- The pace of organizational life makes it inconvenient for others to deliver timely, direct feedback to New Leaders.

- The prevailing organizational belief is that people who need feedback "don't get it," and are a bad fit for the organization and role.

- New Leaders are in such a hurry that they don't foster transparent conversations.

- Overconfident people may not recognize the importance of feedback, and may not request or welcome it. Behaving this way may alienate others and train them to withhold needed feedback.

- Someone who works closely with a New Leader may be unhappy about their appointment, and resulting negative emotion can turn into destructive behavior, including withholding crucial information (see chapter IX on rivals).

- Leaders with low self-awareness may simply not understand their impact on others, or not care.

- People may be too nice, and not want to hurt a New Leader's feelings (this is especially true in the US's Midwest region).

- Perhaps a New Leader is different from others in the organization in some visible way (gender, nationality, race, or sexual orientation). Unfortunately, but still frequently true, some differences may make it difficult to connect, build relationships, and gain access to honest, helpful feedback.

Without the information they need to effectively navigate, New Leaders can "crash and burn." An unfortunate, and often avoidable, reality. It can be especially difficult for New Leaders to gain accurate feedback from their direct reports.

The Gift of Navigational Tools

You have probably heard someone say, "feedback is a gift." For the well being of organizations and their New Leaders, it is crucial to provide early, specific feedback about the effectiveness of their transitions. With that knowledge, New Leaders can successfully navigate—make better decisions, gain needed support for change initiatives, course-correct, and become firmly woven into the organizational fabric.

Some options for stimulating the delivery of feedback include:

- Helping New Leaders understand why they were chosen for the role, so they can fully grasp how their strengths and weaknesses are viewed. (This will also give them a more balanced perspective of themselves during their transition, as organizations often share only positive interview feedback with candidates and new hires.)

- Focusing on building strong relationships with key stakeholders, and asking them for feedback early and often. Creating a pattern of regular open communication will make it easier for stakeholders to share their greatest concerns with the New Leaders, during and after their transition.

- Providing New Leaders with a *Culture Snapshot* (see page 171), so they can make accurate appraisals of the effectiveness of their operations. This also serves to help others in the operation feel like they are receiving fair and balanced feedback about their effectiveness, and not simply the judgment of the Leader (who is too new to form an accurate, comprehensive understanding).

- Facilitating a *Team Alignment Process* (see page 172), where New Leaders receive anonymous, powerful feedback from their direct reports. Extending the focus beyond the New Leader's transition behaviors affords them a more precise view into the team and organizational context. The New Leader and team can then identify meaningful action they can take together to align their efforts and improve their effectiveness.

- Delivering data from *LevelSet: Early Feedback* (see page 171) when New Leaders have been in their role for only six to eight weeks (while the window of judgment is still open). Armed with this confidential and anonymous source of feedback, they can course-correct on one or more of over 30 behaviors that are predictive of long-term success.

- Ensuring that the New Leader functions in a way that encourages ongoing feedback, demonstrating acceptance and resulting behavior change.

Seeking, being open to, and acting on feedback are essential elements of New Leader success. With a clear picture of how their actions and perceptions impact the organization, New Leaders have the tools to maintain their equilibrium, successfully navigate the organizational landscape, and avoid getting caught in the window of judgment, as it slams shut.

Are New Leaders Hearing from Direct Reports?

"The major reason people don't give the boss feedback is they're worried that the boss will retaliate because they know that most of us have trouble accepting negative feedback," says Linda Hill, the Wallace Brett Donham Professor of Business Administration at Harvard Business School. . . . While you may be tempted to enjoy this deference, the silence will not help you, your organization or your career.

From "How to Get Feedback When You're the Boss" by Amy Gallo[3]

Your Keys to Gathering and Providing Feedback to the New Leader

What the Hiring Manager can do.

- Support the New Leader's transition by making resources available to obtain the kinds of feedback provided by the navigational tools listed in this chapter. Be sure to engage the

HR Partner in this process, whether the resources are delivered by an internal or external expert.

- Develop a cadence for providing feedback to the New Leader: both positive and corrective, shared as valuable information (rather than expression of disappointment), and done in a timely fashion. Be clear about role expectations, and then use feedback as an opportunity to reinforce those requirements.

What the New Leader can do.

- Seek out feedback early and often (and informally) from a variety of stakeholders. Use your "meet and greets" as a forum for defining how you will communicate in the future, accompanied by a request that they reach out whenever they either need something or have valuable feedback to share. Then reward your colleagues for doing so by thanking them and demonstrating a positive response to the information shared.

- Where possible, also engage in more structured feedback opportunities (such as the navigational tools outlined in this chapter). These will be most effective if the information is provided anonymously, and you respond in confidence. Making it safe for those downstream of you to provide needed information should be a priority.

What the HR Partner can do.

- Build a positive relationship with the New Leader as early as possible. Work to help them see you as a trusted confidante and sounding board. Stay somewhat detached, and let the New Leader bring their observations to you, rather than you giving them a comprehensive briefing about the history and context of their operation.

- Keep your ear to the ground for informal or "grapevine" feedback about how effectively the New Leader is navigating the role. Where appropriate, share general themes with the

New Leader (provided you see the comments substantiated). It is always helpful to connect the New Leader with more objective and private opportunities for feedback (see navigational tools on page 171). If they choose to share the resulting confidential data with you, that's a plus—but it shouldn't be required.

XI

Evolving the New Leader's Team
Sizing Up, Investing In, or Trading Out

When New Leaders enter an organization, or advance by way of internal promotion, they often inherit a team to lead. Undoubtedly, stepping in as the New Leader can create a wave of concern—and even fear—among direct reports. In the current business climate, it's not unusual to see a new CEO or VP "clean house" and start over with a hand-picked team (often people already known to the New Leader).[1] But is this "revolving door" approach really the best course of action?

While navigating the onboarding process, New Leaders often need to evaluate and address concerns about their assigned teams. Three typical approaches are:

1. The wait-and-see method—studying how team members react to the New Leader's direction.

2. The trade-out approach—rapidly replacing most or all of the individuals on the team.

3. Active involvement—connecting with team members, reviewing their work portfolio, and asking them about the

organization, their internal partners, career aspirations, and their opinions of current operations.

Sizing Up: Know Your Team Before Making A Move

So, which tactic is most appropriate to the situation? To answer this, New Leaders must make a conscientious effort to accurately size up their teams while considering the organizational context. With our clients, we promote the active-involvement approach (number three listed in the previous paragraph), and suggest these 10 steps for New Leaders as they enter their roles:

1. Communicate that they have been hired to maintain operations and generate results.

2. Paint a powerful picture of the future that doesn't denigrate past efforts (and identifies past efforts as foundational to future success).

3. Reassure team members that they are all invited to be part of the future, and include them on the journey.

4. Invite each team member to meet privately, sharing a portfolio of the work they are most proud of. Ask them to share their career objectives, plus strengths, weaknesses, and current capability development activities. Focus on the positive, and avoid sharing any concerns you may have about them/their performance.

5. Use a variety of data points and perspectives to determine the capability and capacity of team members individually, and as a whole.

6. Match up organizational needs with the talent available on the team—analyze strengths and fill gaps.

7. Explore the organization's culture and existing expectations about developing or replacing team members.

8. Get advice from trusted colleagues (but avoid acting solely on others' perceptions).

9. Determine the financial and operational impact of retaining, evolving, or changing the team.

10. Gain support from key others for decisions made about the team.

Key Areas New Leaders Should Evaluate When Sizing Up Their Teams[2]

Criteria to Consider	Questions to Ask
Skills	• Do the combined skills on the team match up with your strategy? • Are there any needed skills missing on the existing team? • Can team members learn new skills if required?
Competencies	• Can you move team members around to increase effectiveness? • Can the current team meet the demands of a new strategy? • Is the team balanced, or are changes needed?
Knowledge	• Do you need a deeper understanding of the area you now manage? • Are they willing to share that knowledge? • Are team members willing to learn different ways of operating?

If told by others that their team is low-performing, New Leaders might be tempted to quickly choose the trade-out approach. An organization may even "suggest" such a move, and request that it be done before the New Leader completes their due diligence. However, acting without examining these situations closely, can lend to costly results[3]—on both financial and personal levels. New Leaders confronted with this dilemma should consider exploring the following questions:

- Why is the team perceived as low-performing?

- Does the organizational (or role) structure support effective performance?

- Does the team have access to the needed tools, knowledge, feedback, and training?

- Has the team experienced multiple leadership changes (or long gaps without a leader) over a short period of time?

- Have prior leaders explained and clarified performance expectations, providing support and resources needed for high performance?

- Are there any documented issues related to individual or team integrity?

Investing In: Is It a Risk or Reward?

Taking time to answer the above questions can help New Leaders determine if team-performance issues emanate from the members of the team themselves, or if factors outside of their influence are the root cause of the problem. If it is the latter, then replacing the team will not improve effectiveness. In his article, "Taking Over from an Incompetent Team Leader," Roger Schwarz states, "Team members' knowledge and skills may be masked by the dysfunctional structures, processes, and expectations that the previous leader created and within which team members operate."[4] In fact, the time and knowledge lost to replacing team members are likely to cost far more than the benefits offered by trade-outs. Knowing this, New Leaders can then focus on the best path for results— addressing the structure and context in which they work.

Once New Leaders decide to invest in their current teams, a good starting point is creating and/or strengthening alignment to ensure team members are set up for success. This includes advocating needed resources, defining work, distributing tasks in ways that make sense, and demonstrating that the New Leader values the team's performance. This fosters cohesion within the team and provides a message of alignment to important others. To reinforce this alignment, New Leaders must also communicate their belief that the team will have a significant positive performance impact, and identify behaviors that will lead to continued improvements.

When New Leaders define the context for their team's goals and articulate and align expectations, their entire team works together more fluidly. New Leaders who foster a climate of transparency and open communication are better-equipped to foster collaboration and build unity. Such cohesion is only possible through unearthing, exposing and resolving past or present barriers to success.

> It's important that the new leader communicate norms and expectations. Until he and his team calibrate norms and expectations, they may be operating under very different assumptions. People approach work differently and every new leader has to make explicit his approach and expectations.
>
> From *Assimilating New Leaders: The Key to Executive Retention*[5]

Trading Out: When Is It Necessary?

New Leaders should fully invest in understanding their operation and employees when evolving the team. And before considering the removal of an individual, New Leaders benefit from adopting best practices in team development. Those include following due process in understanding the team, building support for the desired end state, articulating where the New Leader is going, and inviting everyone on the team to go along. (The clear exception is when a team member is found to have engaged in unethical or illegal behavior.)

By design, a new atmosphere of clarity and alignment may reveal individual team members who are not able (or willing) to get on track with agreed-upon direction and goals. These people often avoid adopting needed changes—they may state how things "should" operate, or may be unwilling to give up their unproductive methods. These rare inflexible members of the team may (knowingly or inadvertently) hinder the team's progress. Certainly, some do come around, and all should be given encouragement and the opportunity to do so. But once New Leaders offer a fair number of opportunities to gain team member buy-in and receive only opposition, a trade-out may need to be considered.

Removing a team member doesn't always require that they also leave the organization. It does mean, however, that this member has skills or behaviors that no longer meet the needs of the team. Successful New Leaders help these team members surface this misalignment for themselves, and then support them in finding suitable alternative opportunities, whether internal or external. Most importantly, the New Leader's commitment to interpersonal due process signals to others that they are taking a thoughtful and fair approach. Being fair builds the foundation for trust and future team (and New Leader) effectiveness.

Evolving the Team: It Comes Down to Discernment and Effort

Addressing a team's viability is just one aspect in a multi-faceted onboarding process. How the New Leader approaches decisions about an inherited team can lead to either early success or delayed disaster. New Leaders should use caution when a Hiring Manager suggests or directs that the team "must go." Taking the active-involvement approach will strengthen the team, prevent disruption, save valuable time, and protect the bottom line.

Dean's Story

I hired Dean to take on a high-end leadership role in our manufacturing company. I felt confident about my choice in Dean, but also knew he would face some trials along the way. He not only uprooted his family and moved 500 miles to a city and company where he knew few people, but he also replaced a 35-year veteran of the organization, who had spent 20 years in the same senior position.

Starting out, I told Dean that his primary goal was to initiate needed changes, and warned him that this organization that was pretty set in its ways (and generally undisciplined). Also, his direct reports were rather unsettled at Dean's arrival, as he represented the unknown—but expected—change.

Dean quickly realized that his inherited team was in disarray—performance was substandard and turnover was high. He admitted to me that he was tempted to proceed with widespread terminations, saying, "I came from a culture where it was commonplace to 'blow up' parts of the organization whenever change was needed." I could understand his impatience, but I thought that type of change might be a bit too drastic. In response I suggested, "Let's look at some options for approaching this before we make any moves."

On my advice Dean agreed to meet with one of our onboarding coaches, and after some conversation, he became open to a different transition strategy.

Dean decided that instead of cleaning house he would start by meeting regularly with his team. In these meetings he clearly defined his vision, including a step-by-step action plan that articulated what each team member would need to do to drive that change. After that, he invited everyone on the team to commit to the journey—to get on board.

As Dean worked to evolve his team, he demonstrated respect for the existing corporate culture—all while moving the organization forward as a change agent. This process helped Dean and his team trust each other. He soon began to understand the fears his team had about him, as well as their true capability and potential.

As a result, Dean's department achieved significant early performance goals (including a double-digit increase in sales) which were broadly recognized by upper management. To sustain this growth, Dean developed a mentoring culture that increased retention, raised skill levels, and helped in recruiting additional high-performing candidates. His team has continued to drive improved financial performance over the last 10 years.

Your Keys to Evolving the New Leader's Existing Team

What the Hiring Manager can do.

- Be clear about deliverables and expectations for the New Leader and team. That consistency will allow your new hire to truly understand their role, and establish alignment with their team members.

- Keep the New Leader focused on understanding the culture and context in which their new team operates. While you hired this New Leader to bring best practices, they need to proceed deliberately enough to set aside preconceived notions about talent and solutions until they have developed strong foundational knowledge about their new operation.

What the New Leader can do.

- Resist the temptation to rapidly size up and reconfigure your team. In certain cases (emergencies, or clear-cut integrity issues), this may be required. However, in most transitions you would be well-advised to take 60 to 90 days to objectively size up the team and operation.

- Remember to make the distinction between what you perceive as your team's capabilities, and the extent to which their roles and context currently allow them to fully perform. Most employees come to work with the intention of making a positive contribution—and your job is to remove barriers and set the context for their success.

What the HR Partner can do.

🟊 Be a true business partner, with a strong understanding of the business strategy and how the New Leader's operation must perform to meet expectations. Even if you have faced challenges with team members, try to avoid briefing the New Leader about those individuals. Instead, allow the New Leader to evaluate them objectively. (In struggling operations, poor performance can often be traced back to the prior leader's management style and treatment of their team members.)

🟊 After the New Leader has taken enough time to size up their team members, introduce them to the organization's talent planning process. Identify criteria and methods for formally assessing team members, and work with the New Leader to visually array current skill/potential levels. Then share past talent planning data, describing each team member's previous and current skill development priorities and activities relative to the New Leader's findings.

XII

Personal Style
How It Affects Perceptions of New Leader "Fit"

In order to be effective, New Leaders should first step back and study the organization they are entering (and the people in it). Unfortunately, for a variety of reasons, some New Leaders dive headlong into a role without thinking about the impact their actions may have on others. Oblivious New Leaders do so at their own peril, failing to meet the needs and expectations of key individuals around them.

The results: angry and resentful colleagues, neglected direct reports, and a Hiring Manager who wonders if the right selection decision was made. Not a great way to start a new job. Damaged relationships can ultimately lead to a New Leader's undoing, and it will reinforce the idea that somehow they weren't the right "fit" for the organization.

From Self-Awareness to Success

There is a better way to navigate the onboarding process than the white-knuckle approach. New Leaders must develop self-awareness about their own leadership style, and address the needs of key others in the organization. During their transition, they can access a variety of tools designed to foster self-understanding about style. Our favorite is the Myers-Briggs Type Indicator (MBTI). The MBTI is an established self-assessment that is respected, non-clinical, straightforward, and the results are easy to interpret. It provides a quick view into how people perceive the world and make decisions (which ultimately directs one's behavior), and it offers a widely-understood framework for leader transition effectiveness.

Jessica's Story

As a first time General Manager, I led a manufacturing company that had fallen into significant disrepair. Employees were working in poor conditions, and they were visibly unhappy. Our operation hadn't turned a profit in over two years. Being the "typical" ESTJ, I was amped up, ready for the challenge, and excited to turn things around.

The plant was owned by a larger holding company located in another state, so I relied on weekly conference calls to keep long-distance peers and leadership informed. However, I started getting feedback that those meetings were not going as well as I had hoped.

Sensing tension with my employer, I met with an onboarding coach and shared, "People at the plant are getting excited about our new vision. I talk to line staff as much as I can—to see how they are doing, what they need, and I ask for their ideas on improving operations. As a result, we've already seen an increase in attendance and productivity."

"But," I paused, "in my weekly conference calls with corporate, I feel like I'm talking to a brick wall. I provide details, and fill them in on employee morale by sharing stories. This is what they hired me to do, and I thought they would be equally excited to hear about our progress. However, I just get cold responses. Honestly, sometimes I think they're annoyed, and I'm not sure what's causing this disconnect."

The coach thought for a moment, and then responded, "It seems like you are working in two different worlds. One (in your plant) is an interactive world where camaraderie and relationships are valued. The other (at corporate) is a more minimalistic one that revolves on efficiency, directness and numbers. To be successful in both areas you need to interact differently with the culture upstream. Adapt your communication style to theirs."

My coach was right. I stopped including narratives in the corporate meetings. Instead I used basic "headlines"— giving brief reports, and then inviting them to request more details if needed. It was awkward at first, but I finally felt like they were listening and responding. Ironically, sharing fewer details seemed to pique their interest in our progress even more.

As an ESTJ, I struggled with this change because I couldn't tell the whole story of our transition. With some practice the interactions with my corporate colleagues became more comfortable every week. And it paid off. Within six months the plant was restored to profitability, morale increased, and my peers now consider me a go-to colleague and leader.

New Leaders who use the MBTI assessment tool should keep in mind that the results are indeed reflective of their preferences, and not necessarily the "right" way of seeing and doing things. In addition, the survey should be completed thinking not about how they function in the workplace, but instead focusing on their natural state.

MBTI measures preferences in four key dimensions. Which of the item descriptors resonate more and seem truest for you?

1. Source of energy: are you motivated more through interactions with others, or recharged by solitude?

2. Information and data gathering: are you more interested in numbers and sequential data, or are you likely to cast a

broader net, seeking a variety of information (external in-
puts, qualitative information, etc.)?

3. Decision making: do you have steadfast rules of thumb to
maintain consistency, or are you more concerned about
the impact your decisions may have on individuals?

4. Planning and implementation: are you structured and time-
bound in planning, or do you embrace a more spontane-
ous and flexible approach?

MBTI and Your New Role

At this point, you may be asking, "What does any of this have to
do with my transition as a New Leader?" The answer is simple. By
applying what you discover about your preferences (and behavior)
within your new work context, you can increase your chance of
onboarding success. As your career progresses, the stakes change—
it is not enough to work hard. According to Marshal Goldsmith
and Mark Reiter, authors of *What Got You Here Won't Get You There*,
"The higher you go, the more your problems are behavioral."[1]

How might each of the four dimensions play out in the actions
and expectations of your new colleagues (and the broader organizational culture)? What are the risks of rigidly holding to your own
preferences? How can you pick your "battles" wisely, so you can
choose to better-adapt (instead of asserting what you think is best)?
We often tell our clients that as a New Leader you don't have be a
perfect stylistic match to your colleagues. The key to success is
knowing where to adjust your behavior and learning to relate to
others in a positive, productive way.

In this section we will look at all the dimensions of MBTI preferences and how they can influence a New Leader's transition.

Extraversion Vs. Introversion (E/I)

This dimension explores the primary source of energy (and thus
orientation) of individuals. Extraverts draw sustenance from people
and interactions, while Introverts are more likely to feel refreshed

and energetic after time spent alone. As you might imagine, New Leader transitions can be a time of high people interaction, so it may be helpful to optimize onboarding effectiveness through self-awareness. (Important to note: the E/I dimension does not measure shyness—that is an inherent trait that can apply to both Introverts and Extraverts.)

Life Inside the Role

Once hired, both Extraverts and Introverts benefit by adopting behaviors that are included in the range of possibilities for this dimension. New colleagues want to feel liked, understood, and respected. They want New Leaders to value existing practices and historical precedents. Naturally, that involves listening, but it also requires enough approachability for the New Leader's peers and direct reports to let down their guard and share potentially negative feedback and surface problems. The key is to interact in a way that inspires trust and connectedness.

Successful Behavior In the Role	E	I
Asks focused questions, and listens to peers and direct reports.		✓
Expresses thoughts in a personable way, and is viewed as approachable.	✓	
Perceived as transparent and open, and brings an extensive network into the role.	✓	
Develops nuanced interpersonal relationships – is truly interested in getting to know new colleagues.		✓

Advice for Both E and I Leaders: Relax—You're Right for the Role

First of all, be honest with yourself—about who you are, and where you are more comfortable when it comes to communicating and relationship building. No one has the "perfect" preference for the role or for effective onboarding. Your success will depend upon finding the balance between leveraging your strengths and focusing on areas where you need to actively compensate for your preferred approach.

Introverts might benefit from making a conscious effort to demonstrate warmth by adding a personal tone in their conversations. On the other hand, Extraverts should focus on slowing down, listening carefully, and learning from their new colleagues and direct reports. Introverts become more effective when they remember to express their thoughts more frequently, while Extraverts may benefit from taking an active-listening approach. For example, Extraverts (who are often known as "external processors" and tend to think out loud) can signal they are listening by taking notes during conversations.

This high-level view of the challenges faced by Extraverts and Introverts in new roles certainly includes many more nuanced details than the information contained here. And it is definitely worth the consideration of any Leader starting a new role.

Ineffective Behavior Pitfalls
Avoid these missteps

E	I
• Interrupting others and not listening.	• Withholding opinions or ideas.
• Overlooking the search for information needed to make effective decisions.	• Appearing cold and uninterested in others.
• Moving too quickly, missing valuable input from colleagues.	• Being perceived as unapproachable.

Sensor Vs. Intuitor (S/N)

The S vs. N dimension indicates how one identifies, takes in and interprets data, which in turn can influence transition behavior. Sensors tend to be detail-oriented and linear, valuing facts and historical precedents. Intuitors are more likely to interact with data in a less structured way, often thinking about the future more creatively and on a generalized or large scale.

You have probably heard the saying "Can't see the forest for the trees," which is particularly relevant to the S vs. N dimension. Sensors may have a tendency to see individual trees, examine the bark on their trunks, and study their height and symmetry. On the other hand, Intuitors would tend to see, well, a forest.

Leading the Team

Sensors and Intuitors may have different approaches to leading a team. Because they place high value on data and details, Sensors can inadvertently signal mistrust by asking a greater number of questions, or getting too closely involved with parts of the operation normally entrusted to others. (Direct reports are most often impacted this way.)

Conversely, Sensors can also provide specific information and directions to their direct reports—guidance that can create focus and role clarity. And they may be more likely to emphasize following established rules and procedures, which creates greater consistency for the team.

On the other side of the spectrum, Intuitors might distance themselves too much from specifics, and miss opportunities to understand data. They may be more laissez faire about established rules and procedures, which can both increase flexibility and confuse team members. Intuitors may also be more likely to provide vague or confusing directions. However, Intuitors often have the ability to see the big picture, generate original ideas and strategies, and communicate their vision to others.

Successful Behavior With Team	S	N
Provides very specific guidance to team, including necessary details.	✓	
Team members are likely to view them as dependable and knowledgeable.	✓	
Able to generate ideas quickly and encourage creativity on the team.		✓
Can see a vision and articulate it.		✓

Advice for S and N Leaders

If you are new to your role, consider which side of the S/N fence you lean on. Look at how you interact not just with data, but with colleagues and direct reports. Are you missing important details? Or are you intrusively digging into aspects of the operation that are capably managed by others?

Sensors, be sure to communicate why you need to be so deeply involved. It is best to inform direct reports that as part of your learning process you need to ask many questions, often about precedents, policies, and procedures that may be out of your purview. Communicate that you will simply be sizing up the fine points of their work at the beginning of your role, so that you can get to know the responsibilities of each team member better. And then promise to back away as you confirm that everything is operating as it should be. Do provide the caveat that you may dive back into the details if you have concerns after learning more. Then invite team members to reach out to clarify what those issues might be if they see this behavior from you. Remember to follow through on that agreement, even though you may be tempted at times to do deep dives to satisfy your curiosity.

Intuitors are likely to be more distant from the details, and often don't scrutinize the work of their team members as closely.

Because of this, Intuitors could be viewed by some (particularly, strong Sensors) as unprepared or "loosey-goosey." To demonstrate your ability to support success, take a structured approach to communicating, and make time to specifically understand and inform others about organizational metrics. Learn the company acronyms, memorize names, and study precedents, policies, and processes related to your area.

Any balancing act can be accompanied by discomfort of some kind. Going against the grain of your natural inclinations may take some effort and forbearance. And Sensors/Intuitors need to be aware of the impact that their natural preferences have upon their work, the people around them, and their ultimate success. Honor your preference, but also realize that in a leadership role you will need to rein in or counterbalance any extreme ways of thinking and behaving.

Ineffective Behavior Pitfalls
Avoid these missteps

S	N
• Making team members feel mistrusted by micromanaging. • Dodging innovation by saying "no" too quickly, or being too rooted in the facts. • Diminishing the value of creativity on the team.	• Distancing self from necessary details, and failing to see hard facts. • Appearing incompetent and unprepared. • Making assumptions (and decisions) before analyzing data.

Thinker Vs. Feeler (T/F)

The T vs. F dimension is related to how we make decisions. Thinkers use logic and they value consistency when facing a decision. Feelers can come across as more empathetic, and encourage situational fairness in the decision-making process.

Leading Organizational Change

New Leaders often step into a role confronted with a directive from their Hiring Manager to initiate changes. And when faced with this expectation, Thinkers and Feelers are likely to react to this accountability differently.

Thinkers are apt to lean toward logic in this arena. They may see an obvious problem in the organization and believe that it should be repaired immediately. As logical, goal-oriented individuals, Thinkers will analyze the facts, look at data and draw their own conclusions. Once a decision is made by the New Leader, the next step is most often implementation. This linear way of operating usually produces faster action while implementing change.

Feelers tend to consider the history and culture of an organization and the impact of the decision on its members when they see areas that need restructuring. Using a more democratic approach, Feelers will seek input from those impacted by any alterations, and demonstrate that they value these contributions. Even if it takes more time to act, Feelers believe this step of offering interpersonal due process is important. And if time allows for this approach, it can lead to more effective decisions and actions.

Successful Behavior In Leading Change	T	F
Desires consensus, seeks out input from those in the organization.		✓
Can drive needed changes quickly.	✓	
Understands how change may impact people in the organization on a personal level.		✓
Demonstrates a strong sense of logic in making decisions.	✓	

Advice for T and F Leaders

The behavior associated with preferences of both Thinkers and Feelers can add value to any organization. But if one is sitting too close to either end of the spectrum, trouble may ensue. When it comes to leading change, Thinkers and Feelers have a responsibility to examine what is best for the organization. Is it more important to fix an existing problem now? Or, is it better to gather input from various levels to gain support and avoid alienating your peers and direct reports? Should strict rules of thumb be used broadly in decision-making, or does each area impacted by the decision need to be considered separately?

Thinkers risk losing support for their change agency when they try to pluck the "low hanging fruit"—independently solving obvious problems. If you are in this position, remember that there is a reason this area of ineffectiveness has been allowed to perpetuate. The culture may support its existence, and a specific leader might even be responsible for creating the problem. Solicit feedback from others about the changes you want to make—even for seemingly easy modifications. Encourage involvement from your colleagues to build the relationships you need to foster more broadly.

Feelers can help others gain a sense of importance (and stake in the decision) by asking for input. But how far can and should this democracy go? It is usually the right move to solicit some kind of feedback (especially as a New Leader learning the culture), but at what cost? Does the culture see this kind of inclusion as an indicator of New Leader weakness or strength? Keep in mind that timing should also be considered when implementing change. Remember to create some emotional distance when choices need to be made quickly. Otherwise, missed opportunities or blowback may create turmoil in your onboarding process. And learning to separate emotions from decisions (if done in a balanced way) can increase your credibility among peers.

Knowing when and how to face change in a new role is no easy task. It takes effort and understanding for both Thinkers and Feelers. And interactions between Thinker and Feeler colleagues can be smoothed out by understanding your own preference, and recognizing that you need to work to be objective in understanding how you and others relate to change.

Ineffective Behavior Pitfalls Avoid these missteps	
T	**F**
• Being rigid and overly confrontational. • Excluding others' input from decision-making. • Fixing a problem too quickly without understanding the culture/people impact.	• Reacting emotionally to differences of opinion. • Allowing emotions to cloud decision-making. • Requesting input from everyone to a point where progress is often delayed.

Judger Vs. Perceiver (J/P)

So far, we have examined how preferences and behaviors associated with Extraversion/Introversion, Sensor/Intuitor, and Thinker/Feeler dimensions impact New Leader transitions. We conclude the discussion by considering how Judger/Perceiver behaviors can influence a New Leader's onboarding experience, and how to manage the risks associated with each approach.

The Judger/Perceiver dimension describes how individuals relate to time and the need to structure and plan their work—ranging from the kickoff of a planning process to goal execution. This is an important dimension to consider because every organization (and workgroup) has different cultural norms about timeliness, planning, and execution.

Judgers tend to be proactive about planning, and build structure around their deliverables to ensure their work is delivered in a timely and orderly fashion. They are also more likely to arrive at meetings early (or on time). Perceivers are inclined to leave their options open, not becoming too locked into one path to an outcome; and they are better able to adapt to unexpected circumstances.

Driving Performance

Judgers and Perceivers need to look before they leap, and understand that taking action happens most effectively after sizing up the organization. As you might imagine, Judgers and Perceivers are likely to have different approaches to driving change, and should challenge themselves to flex between J and P mode throughout. Once they understand their new operation, New Leaders are now in a position to take action—why else would they be there?

Managing daily performance will likely differ between Judgers and Perceivers. Judgers have an urgency to gain closure and may quickly jump into the fray. They might generate a strategy and have goals in place even before their nameplate is ordered. Judgers tend to find comfort in creating order, defining steps, and holding themselves and others accountable for follow-through. You won't catch Judgers or their teams racing to meet a deadline. They are decisive, deliberate, and if they anticipate any potential changes, they will plan accordingly. Conversely, when unexpected changes occur, Judgers might struggle to adjust, and could be viewed as not having considered enough possibilities before taking action.

Perceivers are more likely to cast a broad net in their aspirations for the operation—to see what is possible. They enjoy the freedom to carve their own path and "go with the flow," and may create a work environment that fosters this approach. Those with this preference tend to take risks by "thinking outside the box," which can be essential to the organization's success. Perceivers are comfortable in more ambiguous settings where ample time allows them to consider their next step, and they can adapt to changes without much concern. But this can negatively impact the team's ability to deliver results in a timely way (and frustrate those who prefer a structured, well-communicated approach).

Successful Behavior In Performance Management	J	P
Will hold themselves and others accountable.	✓	
Willing to take needed risks without all the answers in place.		✓
Mastery of deadlines, decisive, and organized, they will get the job done.	✓	
Can "go with the flow" and demonstrate flexibility with their approach.		✓

Advice for J and P Leaders

Both Judgers and Perceivers are an asset to any organization. The key for both types of New Leaders is to understand which behaviors the organization values, apply their strengths, and develop strategies for overcoming challenges.

Judgers naturally strategize, recognize the organization's direction and advance in a systematic way. However, it is often the case that tested methods are not the best choice—new challenges may require new solutions. Increasing flexibility while retaining your goal-setting skills can make you a balanced and appreciated New Leader. With this in mind Judgers should:

- Anticipate that in every kind of role, curve balls will be thrown at you and your operation.

- Recognize that structure and planning are important, but too much of either can stifle progress.

- Give others in your organization time to catch up to you, and respect their need for freedom to think creatively and respond flexibly.

- Realize that becoming agile will likely require some letting go of the original plan.

On the other end of the spectrum, Perceivers should understand that their agility and strength in risk-taking can also greatly benefit the organization. And making an effort to combine broad-band thinking with a more-structured approach will make your risk-taking side look intentional, instead of just lucky. To get there we suggest that Perceivers:

- Know that goals will need to be set, and deadlines met.

- Realize that those around you will require clarity on your direction.

- Read the signals—if work is piling up, it's time to approach your work differently.

- Demonstrate accountability for yourself and others, and respect (and support) others' need to bring projects or work processes to closure.

Ineffective Behavior Pitfalls
Avoid these missteps

J	P
▪ Reacting negatively to unexpected changes or circumstances. ▪ Forcing decisions before interpersonal due process is satisfied. ▪ Avoiding risks by using only black-and-white thinking.	▪ Appearing indecisive and disorganized even with a strong knowledge base. ▪ Procrastinating and allowing work to pile up. ▪ Generating plans too slowly or ambiguously.

Understanding your preferences and how they relate to the onboarding experience can smooth your entry into a new role and work environment. Thinking proactively about your MBTI profile, especially as it relates to your new culture and team, allows you to lead more flexibly and become more relevant to your new operation.

Recommended Reading

For those wishing to expand their knowledge of how MBTI preferences impact the role of leaders in an organization, we suggest reading the following publications.

- *Type Talk at Work* by Otto Kroeger and Janet M. Thuesen
- *The Introverted Leader* by Jennifer B. Kahnweiler, PhD
- *Please Understand Me: Character and Temperament Types* by David Keirsey and Marilyn Bates
- *The Heart of Change: Real-Life Stories of How People Change Their Organizations* by John P. Kotter and Dan S. Cohen

Your Keys to Leveraging MBTI Preferences

What the Hiring Manager can do.

- Avoid the temptation to hire "against type" in order to drive needed change. Too often, hiring decisions are made in favor of leaders who have fundamentally different styles from the prevailing culture or the previous incumbent (particularly in fix-it or turnaround situations). Instead, probe for adaptability—the tendency to modulate behavior based on the requirements of the situation. Most importantly, <u>do</u> <u>not</u> use the MBTI as a selection process assessment tool, as it is not a validated, legally defensible way of choosing the most qualified candidate for the role.

- Understand your own MBTI preference as you learn about your new direct report. Recognize that just because someone leads differently than you do doesn't make them "wrong" in actions and decisions (conflicts in style can happen across all four dimensions). Consider having a very open conversation with your new hire about your respective MBTI preferences, and identify ways that the two of you can both actively bridge differences. Acknowledge that being similar also carries risks, particularly of groupthink or incomplete consideration of alternative paths of decisions.

What the New Leader can do.

❧ Know yourself, and your MBTI preferences well. Consider how your clear preferences could lead to overdone strengths, and slight preferences can create confusion (because your resulting situational behavior is less predictable to others). Consider using the MBTI in a team-building experience, such as the *Team Alignment Process* (see page 172), to help your team more rapidly understand you as a leader. That exercise will also give you greater insight into the motivations and needs of your team members, and allow all to more objectively understand each other.

❧ Use your "meet and greets," as well as broad, ongoing relationship-building, to help you develop a more nuanced understanding of organizational culture (as it pertains to the MBTI). Like humans, organizations have stylistic preferences. When coupled with self-knowledge, you will be armed with navigational tools that can speed and cement your success.

What the HR Partner can do.

❧ Focus on truly getting to know your candidates before recommending hires. Used appropriately, pre-hire assessments can reveal leadership style, and allow you to have informed conversations with final candidates to gauge how effectively they may be able to adapt their approach to the requirements of the new culture and team.

❧ Draw on your familiarity with the MBTI to facilitate a team-building meeting for the New Leader. Work through the four dimensions by asking them to consider the contributions made by those of the other type, as well as ways that people with their own preferences could undermine team effectiveness. Top it off with some behavioral contracting to make all team members accountable for effectively managing less-than-helpful behavior that may naturally stem from their combination of MBTI preferences.

XIII

Don't Underestimate the Importance of the Personal Transition

Landing a senior-level leadership position can be a momentous time in anyone's career. And for executives, many job appointments include changes that impact their personal lives, such as moving to another city, state, or even country. Successfully navigating this aspect of the onboarding process requires intentional adjustments by New Leaders and their families. Almost all New Leaders encounter personal struggles in their transitions, but they may (for a variety of reasons) downplay the hardships they face while acclimating to their new role, organization, and geography. Seeming resilient, while not feeling so, may been seen as a necessary part of a New Leader's role, but we would suggest it is problematic.

Our research with one large retail client demonstrated that the number two predictor of New Leader turnover is the extent to which their personal transitions go poorly. (The number one predictor is failure of New Leaders to achieve and maintain role clarity.) And clients in a variety of other market sectors and geographies have echoed this problem. According to the Society for Human Resources Management, "Employees whose moves go badly, or who conflict with their new bosses or clash with their new loca-tions, can end up leaving the jobs they moved to take. Employers should build solid relocation programs to ... reduce the risk that a botched relocation might push a valued employee to leave."[1]

Employers should consider relocation a significant onboarding risk factor, evaluate elements of the transition most likely to cause difficulty, and develop strategies for providing ongoing support. While many companies have relocation specialists who provide initial assistance for executive moves, it is important to remain at-tentive to this largely invisible part of New Leader transition for at least six months.

What Are the Root Causes of Tricky Personal Transitions?

For most corporate leaders, moving for a new role or promotion is nothing out of the ordinary. But in recent years, we have seen some trends surface in New Leader relocations that may contribute to unexpected derailment or departure. On the following pages we will discuss some of those trends.

New Leaders who have spouses/significant others employed in professional roles.

It is becoming increasingly common for trailing spouses/significant others to seek high-level positions that may be tough to obtain in the new geography. Searching for a job while staying in their pre-move role can also lead to personal fatigue for the trailing spouse, and a drawn-out physical separation. New Leaders must balance the importance of their success with their spouses' and/or significant others' ability to secure employment.[2] Employers often do, or are willing to, provide some form of trailing spouse assis-tance.

Families of New Leaders stay behind for an extended period of time.

New Leaders often go it alone at the beginning of their transi-tion so their children can stay behind to complete the school year.

Although the intention may be to help their children acclimate, some evidence suggests that the longer the family stays behind, the less likely they are to eventually make the actual move. This ongoing connection to the old geography, in turn, increases the chance that New Leaders will leave their new employers to meet the needs and expectations of the family they left behind.

Sometimes New Leaders do not relocate their families at all.

While this used to be "red flag" for HR Partners concerned about retention, it is now more common for New Leaders to rent apartments in the new city and stay during the week—commuting home on the weekend. This seems to be particularly true when their offspring are adolescents, or have grown up and left home.

While it may be helpful to monitor, it's probably most respectful to curb efforts to effect a full relocation. You may, however, want to let the New Leader know that the relocation package remains available for some period of time following their actual start date—leaving room for them to change their mind.

New Leaders and their families often choose to ride out the process of selling their old home.

In recent years, the depressed housing market has extended the time it takes to successfully sell one's home (particularly with homes that have a high price tag). Living in temporary rentals and delaying the purchase of a home adds time to the moving process, can create stress from crowding or inconvenience, and hinders a family's ability to settle in and create a routine. If frustration hits a high point, New Leaders may lack the incentive to fully commit to their new employers by putting down roots locally.

New Leaders may experience greater resistance from children.

As their offspring (particularly adolescents) become involved in high-commitment activities (such as travel sports teams, clubs, and extracurricular activities), New Leaders may encounter unexpectedly strong push-back for a proposed move. In addition, moves are often most stressful when the children are in middle or high school, as they will be severing longtime ties and starting over in a new town. Moving expert, Diane Schmidt, states, "Leaving behind friends, moving to a new school and a new neighborhood is especially hard on this age group."[3] The stronger their emotional distress about such a move, the more likely the teens will be able to exert undue influence upon their parents—thus delaying or preempting a move.

If families are anxious or upset about the move, New Leaders might not lean on them as a source of social support.

Our research demonstrates that the risk of New Leader turnover elevates when family satisfaction with the transition is low. With unhappy households come discontented New Leaders. And they must mask their struggles so as not to compound the issues or unhappiness their families face. This can create (often debilitating) feelings of New Leader isolation.

The families of New Leaders may have deep roots in their existing community.

Families may find their destination different enough to engender feelings of alienation. In addition, the strong relationships left behind that were sources of support and enjoyment are now not as accessible.

New Leaders who are single may have less support available to them during their transition.

Transitioning into a community not known to them, single New Leaders may have a harder time creating relationships outside of work.[4] The basic logistics of a move can be daunting, as well. Being on their own, they may need time off from their organization to be present for cable and phone installation, or to accept delivery of appliances and furniture. And these interruptions can lead to frustration and undermine their satisfaction with the new role.

Global transfers and expatriate assignments can be fraught with unknowns.

Language barriers, cultural differences, and conflicting beliefs about practices important to families (such as religion or raising/educating children) can compound problems. Any challenges that might be faced in a typical domestic relocation may be amplified when it is an international move—trying to find medical providers, childcare, or suitable housing can be frustrating during an already disorienting transition.

The personal impact of these kinds of transitions is often exacerbated due to the general nature of leader transitions. As noted in the graphic below while a New Leader's learning curve tends to be a steady climb, their emotional responses to transition may fluctuate significantly and unpredictably—and over an extended period of time. Leaders who are advised of the potential transition turbulence in advance are more likely to successfully adapt to ups-and-downs (and survive in their roles).

The Emotional and Intellectual Journey

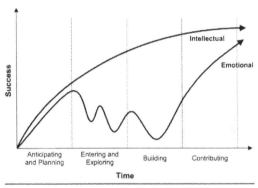

Reprint: Downey, March, and Berkman, 2001[5]

Some Solutions and Coping Strategies

The difficulties New Leaders and their families experience while negotiating an unfamiliar landscape are facts of life that cannot be avoided.[6] Some ideas for New Leader and organization response include:

- **Work together as a family on solutions.**
  Before packing up your belongings, hold a family powwow to identify potential pitfalls and develop strategies. Keep

the focus on the exciting opportunities this move presents, while minimizing (but not ignoring) the challenges. Make a list of enjoyable activities in the destination location, and commit to exploring them early in the move.

- **Allow family members to weigh in on decisions.**
  Take children along to tour one or two area schools so that they can influence final choices. Based on their feedback, families can opt to narrow their housing search to a preferred school district. Offspring can also be enlisted to help design and choose furnishings for their home, particularly the areas where they will entertain friends.

- **Utilize resources available from employers.**
  Large organizations often have trailing-spouse policies that can help them secure employment. If formal support is not offered, many new colleagues will be eager to assist. They can also recommend schools, neighborhoods, and community resources such as doctors, plumbers, tutors, and veterinarians. More informally, colleagues can advise New Leaders about local culture, community events, and include the new families in their own social plans.

- **Draw on strengths from existing relationships while forging new ones.**
  Continue to reach out to family and friends from the former location. Plan one or more trips to see them during the first year, include them in vacation plans, or invite them to visit. Employ communications tools such as video calling software, online chat, and email to preserve these important connections. Good places to initiate new relationships[7] include local houses of worship, children's sports teams, community events and volunteering.[8]

- **Leave right after the school year ends.**
  If New Leaders' families opt to stay behind to finish the school year, it is highly recommended that they depart right after school adjourns for the summer. It may be challenging

for the children initially, but it can be a very effective way to meet peers in the neighborhood, or through summer camps and sporting events. When the school year rolls around in the fall, the children will already have strong foundations in building relationships. And they can avoid the "new kid" anxieties that often accompany these moves.

International Moves and Expatriate Assignments

Being offered permanent roles in a different country (or shorter-term expatriate assignments) can present exciting opportunities for New Leaders and their families. Importantly, perhaps more than any other kind of relocation, it can be fraught with uncertainty and complexity. Some steps to manage these situations include:

1. **Start learning the language.**
   As soon as you know of an assignment to a foreign land immerse the family in lessons. When possible, practice at home over dinner and in other conversations, at local restaurants serving the cuisine of the destination location, and try to make the interactions interesting and fun. Continue those lessons upon arrival.

2. **Familiarize yourselves with the history, habits, and customs of the new geography.**
   Research together as a family, and discuss what these changes will be like. Keep it positive as you share ideas. Find recipes for authentic versions of the country's cuisine, and make them together as a family. Identify geographies and adjacent countries you can take side-trips to, and plan for your first trip before you even make the move.

3. **Think carefully about where you want to live.**
   Many New Leaders and their families prefer expatriate communities where amenities are familiar and their neighbors speak the same native tongue. These families often send their children to international or American schools. Others specifically choose to live outside of those buffered

neighborhoods to immerse themselves into the culture. The choice is a personal one, and it will greatly impact the expatriate experience. There is no "right" or "wrong" decision, only what best-suits your family.

4. Figure out what to do with your "stuff."
For some families, having familiar surroundings that include their own furnishings is important. For others, it may not matter as much. If you need to pare down, take selected items that are symbolically important such as framed photographs, artwork, bedding, stuffed animals, or sports trophies.

5. Develop strategies to decrease homesickness.
Spend time together as a family, and maintain special traditions, routines, and schedules where possible. Look for additional opportunities to use nearby locales as the launch pad for special adventures or vacations. Invite friends and family to visit, and take them along. Given time, many expats overcome the longing for their old lives and capture the excitement and adventure of their newfound country.

Leaders who ignore the risks of personal transitions in the onboarding process do so at their own peril, leaving employment stability and personal relationships hanging in the balance. If New Leaders proactively evaluate and address the personal risk factors involved, they increase satisfaction in their role. And taking the steps necessary to ensure their families' physical and emotional needs are met further stabilizes their own transition by keeping their support system in balance.

Your Keys to Easing a New Leader's Personal Transition

What the Hiring Manager can do.

1 Recognize the symbolic and personal impact you and your family can have on a New Leader's transition. While your

primary relationship may exist in the workplace, serving as a gracious host to the New Leader and their family can provide much-needed reassurance and social support. Enlist your spouse/significant other to be involved in both formal interactions, such as dinner invitations, and more informally as a person who can connect the family to local resources. Provide a thoughtful housewarming gift, and make yourselves available as a resource on an ongoing basis.

♟ Set the expectation that in the first few weeks the New Leader should feel free to block out time to attend to the personal aspects of transition. They will need to address complex logistical details, as well as accompany their children to their new school. Much as the company should attend to potential dissatisfiers in a New Leader's transition into the role at work, empower them to attend to their own family's potential dissatisfiers.

What the New Leader can do.

♟ Have realistic expectations about your transition. Even if this new role represents a significant opportunity, remember that it will be accompanied by ups and downs for both you and your family. Allow family members to fully express concerns, and take a problem-solving approach to addressing them. Try to keep a positive focus, and carve out one-on-one time with each individual family member, so they feel included and important.

♟ Work to keep connections strong with important people from the previous locale while looking for structured ways to embed yourselves in the new community. Remember that this personal onboarding will take time, and it could be a several months until you and your family feel fully embedded in the new locale.

What the HR Partner can do.

- Use the selection process as a means of showing the candidate (and their family) the potential personal benefits of the move. Expose them to community events, schools, churches, and other opportunities to help them imagine their new lives. Where the family may have unusual needs (such as a child with a chronic medical condition, or who is an elite athlete), mobilize your influence to connect them with the best resources available.

- Develop strong relationships with one or two effective realtors, particularly those who offer relocation services that will support the personal transition needs of your New Leaders. Be explicit about the support you expect, and ask your recent hires to evaluate (post-transition) the extent to which these providers met their needs.

XIV

Building OnBoarding Partnerships That Work

As the earlier sections of this book have suggested, New Leaders and their organizations benefit greatly when onboarding is attended to comprehensively and intentionally. Many challenges await the New Leader, and most difficulties can be minimized or mitigated by taking a systematic approach to effectively seating them in their roles. We believe that onboarding is a fifty-fifty proposition, with both the employer and the New Leader taking on equal responsibility for New Leader success.

The Importance of Building Internal Capacity

Based on over 20 years of experience supporting leader transitions, we have found that the most effective onboarding process is one that is owned and supported by the organization. The Hiring Manager and HR Partner play vitally important roles in successful transitions. They deserve access to tools and methodologies that allow them to consistently support New Leader moves to a variety of roles and functions.

Most large employers currently offer some form of onboarding support, though it may vary widely across organizations. This range could extend from basic orientation to intensive executive coaching.

The Hiring Manager's Role

We must not underestimate the importance of involving the Hiring Manager in New Leader transitions, in a structured and intentional way. Frequent, focused communication will help the New Leader become more quickly (and completely) effective in their role. This dialogue provides them an opportunity to understand and align performance expectations held by others, and test their experiences and observations in real-time. Unfortunately, much as with mentoring programs, the impact of the Hiring Manager on the onboarding process is only effective when their involvement is structured and consistent.

Hiring Managers must educate themselves about the unseen, and vitally important, aspects of effective New Leader moves, such as the personal transition (and other risk factors). Hiring Managers have a responsibility to understand the impact their own leadership is having on their new hire, and find a way to make time for regular, transparent interactions. While it may be tempting for an organization to leave Hiring Managers to their own devices, the downside risk exceeds the advantages to doing so. And an important opportunity is missed—failing to guide the New Leader to more rapid, and comprehensive, alignment and success in their role.

The HR Partner's Role

Day-one orientation has been a staple in the workplace for many years, and is almost exclusively handled internally by HR Partners. However, HR Partners need to recognize that orientation programs and onboarding processes are not the same thing. Our experience and research shows that, to be effective, a comprehensive New Leader onboarding realistically takes place over the first four to six months in their role. In addition, true talent development starts before the first day, and continues throughout the New Leader's tenure. So how does an organization develop and maintain a long-term onboarding process for New Leaders that supports the organization's talent management lifecycle? As companies review their talent development procedures, they often choose to outsource some elements of onboarding, while building internal capacity for others. In-house onboarding processes should set goals that support leader onboarding, and coach towards best practices that drive New Leader results. Importantly, if external onboarding coaching is provided for high-level hires, as is common in many companies, it is still the HR organization's responsibility to influence those activities, measure the effectiveness of outcomes, and hold the coaching providers accountable for excellent support.

With the proper preparation and skill base, HR Partners can become highly effective internal onboarding coaches. They can fill an important organizational void, serving a second tier of New Leaders who might not otherwise benefit from an investment in coaching. For example: an external coaching engagement for a director-level hire might be seen as cost-prohibitive.

For onboarding-savvy clients, we recommend building internal coaching capacity. Typically drawn from the HR function, these internal coaches know their organizations (and the players) best, and are already positioned as valued partners with the business. One key benefit to note here—internal coaches can adapt their approaches in ways that fit the organization, are business-relevant, and can be self-managed.

The Organization's Role

In looking at internal capacity, five steps should be considered when building on an onboarding process.

1. **Review existing onboarding practices, and other resources already in place.**
   Many organizations already embrace the need to provide a robust onboarding experience for their New Leaders, and

deliver that experience largely through external coaching (augmented by internal activities such as orientation). In the book, *Successful Onboarding*, Mark Stein and Lilith Christiansen state, "On the most basic level, firms adopting strategic [onboarding] programs have begun to craft seamless first year experiences that, by taking seriously the perspective of new hires, hiring managers, and the enterprise in whole, address the ongoing needs of the business more effectively than ever before."[1]

Creating comprehensive internal processes for onboarding New Leaders is a fairly new concept in many organizations. In our work with clients, we believe that building internal capacity starts at the same place our work does: understanding the organization's onboarding goals, as well as their current practices.

Also, New Leaders and their employers should understand that they both operate as part of the same system and share responsibility for a successful transition; that they must work together for successful integration during this important onboarding period. This starting point will allow for evaluation and augmentation of current onboarding methods.

2. Research and seek input from external sources.
As organizations strive to incorporate effective leader onboarding practices into their internal processes, many learn they have gaps in their knowledge base and understanding. This leads them to look to external sources, seek counsel, and augment their efforts with experienced providers. Outside practitioners and academicians offer the bulk of research and information available to those seeking to learn more about onboarding New Leaders. Three books that can provide a good starting point are *Assimilating New Leaders: The Key to Executive Retention* by Diane Downey, as well as *The First 90 Days* by Michael Watkins, and *Right From the Start* by Dan Ciampa and Michael Watkins.

In this step, organizations can also network with other companies to benchmark best practices, and determine the extent to which this information has application in their current context. When benchmarking, think broadly, rather than limiting focus to those firms in the same industry or geography. Ask those Leaders new to the company about the effective onboarding practices they may have experienced in their past roles.

3. **Understand key elements of internal onboarding.**

As stated in chapter VIII, the most successful onboarding processes focus on three main areas: developing key relationships, building knowledge (about the organization, its business, and the people), and soliciting and acting upon feedback.

In addition, coaching skills are essential items in the toolkit of those constructing a full internal onboarding process. New Leaders often feel isolated, and don't yet know who can be a trusted confidante. A trained onboarding coach can utilize a structured methodology and professional approach to become a resource and sounding board for New Leaders.

As we partner with organizations to build their internal onboarding capacity, we often emphasize the value of taking a risk management approach to New Leader transition. When this is coupled with an assessment of the organization's talent management goals for their New Leaders, onboarding helps unite these two disparate segments of the talent management lifecycle.

As you may have surmised, the level of involvement and investment an organization employs to begin building their internal onboarding capacity is significant, and will ultimately bear fruit—and should be proportionate to the goals you and your organization hold for the success of your New Leaders.

4. Create and implement an onboarding strategy and methodology.

Based on what the onboarding team has learned, it will be ready to frame up an approach to internal delivery of leader onboarding that is customized to the organization's unique needs and resources. To enjoy long-term success, the strategy must support business direction, be endorsed by top leaders, and be accompanied by strong execution.

Best practice in internal onboarding coaching is the use of a defined methodology, with qualified internal coaches, in a limited, specific pilot test. This approach supports the validation of onboarding methodology while leaving room for course-correction, as needed. Rather than having a splashy roll-out, consider laboring over the first few coaching engagements to perfect your onboarding process.

5. Measure the impact.

Once an organization has developed their internal onboarding capacity, it's time to shift the focus to measuring impact. Create short and long-term success metrics for individual New Leaders, as well as the process, overall. Those metrics can range from New Leader feedback about their own experience to some longitudinal objective measure of onboarding "stickiness," such as retention (or, alternately, turnover) of New Leaders.

Feedback, an essential part of any transition, can also serve as an important diagnostic in an enhanced New Leader onboarding process. Traditional 360-degree feedback surveys gauge the effectiveness of a New Leader only after the organization has had long-term exposure to their performance. (Typically, six months is required before requisite familiarity is formed.) *LevelSet: Early Feedback* (see page 171), however, speeds that formal feedback process by measuring early impressions of the New Leader within the first six to eight weeks, using over 30 specific items proven to predict longer-term New Leader success.

As a diagnostic, *LevelSet* results can indicate areas where the New Leader needs additional support, provide evidence that stakeholder expectations might be misaligned, confirm that there are structural challenges in role definition, and assess other areas that can determine New Leader and organizational success. Our firm delivers *LevelSet Facilitator Qualification* (see page 171) to our internal partners. Leaders who receive early feedback and have the means to create and implement an action plan are more likely to thrive during their transition and beyond.

It may seem like a daunting challenge to create internal capacity for onboarding coaching. But the investment pays dividends in New Leader retention and effectiveness.

Your Keys to Building OnBoarding Partnerships

What the Hiring Manager can do.

❦ Actively support the creation of a systemic onboarding process for New Leaders in your organization. Help others see beyond their own preconceived notions of onboarding, moving from thinking of it as orientation to understanding it as a means of embedding New Leaders for ongoing success. Sponsor the onboarding initiative within your HR operation, and advocate across the organization on the basis of the strong business case for such an initiative.

❦ Make a commitment to personally using a structured, consistent approach with your new hires that focuses them on learning about, and demonstrating respect for, their new context. Resist the temptation to pressure the New Leader to move so quickly (or aggressively) that they build barriers to acceptance, eventual success, and longevity. Recognize that unless the operation is in a true emergency, the Leader and team will be better-served by such an approach. If the New Leader is moving too quickly, or driving uninformed change, work with them to set more appropriate expectations (and then hold them to it).

What the New Leader can do.

🏵 Work to understand the organization's approach to onboarding, and honor it. Recognize the vital importance of your Hiring Manager and HR Partner to your success. Plan your transition with their partnership, and enlist their help as providers of feedback and advice. Be open to the activities and information they provide, while balancing those with your own experiences and perceptions.

🏵 Give yourself the time to fully experience your transition, and make best use of the resources available. If your role is unclear, seek out input from your Hiring Manager, HR Partner, or other trusted colleagues—repeatedly. Remember that your job is not to have all the right answers, but to ask all the right questions—at least for the first two to three months.

What the HR Partner can do.

🏵 See onboarding as starting pre-hire, and ensure that the selection process is a suitable, effective beginning for New Leader onboarding. Identify the tools and methodology that will best-support New Leader effectiveness. Remain in close contact with the New Leader and Hiring Manager throughout their first 90 days in role. Challenge yourself to learn about them and their onboarding experience in service of your own development as a leader (and not just as their process partner). If you wish to become an active onboarding coach, prepare yourself fully and learn from every experience.

🏵 Keep an open mind about what onboarding is, and can be, in your organization. Don't try to go it alone, but also avoid the other extreme of over-relying on outside resources in support of New Leader transition. Have a vision for the experience you want New Leaders to have, and continue to build on each success. Each of those individual successes strengthens the business case for future efforts, and will engender greater resource allocation and other forms of organizational commitment to onboarding.

Speaking and Workshops

The authors are available to speak on the topics listed below, as well as others that can also be customized for your organization's needs.

- **The Myth of "Fit": Unlock New Leader Success with High-Impact OnBoarding**
- **Preventing New Leader Failure**
- **Leader OnBoarding = Risk Management**

Visit www.leaderonboarding.com/SpeakerRequest to schedule a workshop or keynote, and for a complete list of all offerings.

About the Authors

Linda Reese is the Managing Partner of *Leader OnBoarding* (www.leaderonboarding.com), a management consulting and coaching firm specializing in fostering the success of newly-placed executives. She has professional training in the field of Industrial and Organizational Psychology, and uses a pragmatic approach in serving as an advisor to senior management.

Her pioneering approach to aligning New Leaders includes the development of *LevelSet: Early Feedback* and the *Culture Snapshot.* These tools help New Leaders achieve greater role clarity and understand where they're hitting and missing the mark (doing so in a way that predicts their success and provides information early enough for needed course-correction).

Since 1990, Linda has been a practicing coach and consultant, working with New Leaders of over 40 companies in healthcare, financial services, manufacturing, and retail sectors. In addition, she currently serves as Board Chair for books4kids2keep—a not-for-profit organization that strives to build personal libraries in the homes of high-need children. Since 2002, the organization has distributed 1.5 million books to over 25,000 children in Central Ohio, in partnership with Half Price Books and Coca-Cola. Prior to these positions, Linda served in corporate and operational leadership roles for a large retailer.

Linda holds a master's degree and PhD from the University of Illinois (Chicago).

Stephanie Henderson is a seasoned consultant with more than 25 years of business experience. For over 10 years she's been working with *Leader OnBoarding* as an onboarding expert and executive coach. Stephanie focuses on combining talent-management strategies with sustainable leader-development processes to assist New Leaders in aligning with their organization and team, and realizing their full potential. In addition, she works directly with organizations throughout their new hire's career lifecycle—beginning with pre-hire assessment through rapid ramp-up—to establish (or build upon existing) onboarding programs that deliver superior business results.

Having held a range of positions in the financial services industry, Stephanie gained expertise in corporate practices, and developed a deep understanding of organizational behavior. Her insider's knowledge of organizational needs, coupled with a belief that people are the engine that drive results, made her a valuable part of the team that developed *LevelSet: Early Feedback* and *Culture Snapshot*.

Stephanie received a master's degree in Organization and Management from Capella University, obtained Senior Professional in Human Resources certification, and is a qualified user of multiple assessment and consulting tools.

For more information on how the coaches and consultants of *Leader OnBoarding* can assist in developing your organization's onboarding capability, or guiding you through an effective onboarding experience, contact us at 877.733.7310, or email us at info@leaderonboarding.com.

Tools and Processes

Several *Leader OnBoarding* tools and processes are mentioned in the text of this book. Below is a brief description of each, and information on how you can learn more about them.

LevelSet: Early Feedback is an online survey tool that gathers data from a select group of raters to understand how effectively an externally hired New Leader is navigating their role. A qualified facilitator delivers results to the New Leader, highlighting behaviors that drive success, and providing insight into correcting missteps. With this knowledge, the New Leader can course-correct early and avoid making mistakes that could derail them.

LevelSet: Internal Moves is a variant of *LevelSet: Early Feedback,* and offers an internally-deployed New Leader a timely, revealing assessment of their early understanding and effectiveness.

LevelSet Facilitator Qualification is the certification process that allows facilitators to capably use the proprietary assessment tools *LevelSet: Early Feedback* and *LevelSet: Internal Moves.*

To learn more about these tools and the qualification process, visit http://leaderonboarding.com/tools/levelset-early-feedback.

Culture Snapshot is an assessment tool designed to align a New Leader's expectations with the reality of their performance climate and organizational culture. A qualified facilitator guides the New Leader through the findings to help them navigate the culture, gain insight into expectations, and focus on areas of their operation that require improvement. *Snapshot* was developed in partnership with Denison Consulting—global experts in culture and leadership. This tool is derived from the *Denison Organizational Culture Survey*, and is applied within the context of leader transition.

More information about *Snapshot* is available at http://leader onboarding.com/tools/culture-snapshot.

Team Alignment Process is an intervention methodology, developed to align New Leaders with their inherited (or restructured) team. Through a series of confidential interviews (by a qualified facilitator) team members share their honest impressions of the New Leader and insights about barriers to alignment and performance. Follow-up consulting addresses themes and issues that surface in the facilitated team meeting. They identify areas of misalignment with the culture, expectations, capabilities, organizational structure, performance requirements, and resource base. This process reduces ambiguities and increases understanding between the New Leader and their team.

Find out more at http://leaderonboarding.com/services/team -alignment-process.

Notes

Chapter I

1. David G. Allen, *Retaining Talent: A Guide to Analyzing and Managing Employee Turnover* (Alexandria, VA: SHRM Foundation, 2008), 15.
2. Charles Handler, "Success with Pre-Hire Assessment Starts with Using the Right Tool at the Right Time," *ERE Media*, November 28, 2012, https://www.eremedia.com/ere/success-with-pre-hire-assessment -starts-with-using-the-right-tool-at-the-right-time.
3. Katherine W. Phillips, "How Diversity Makes Us Smarter," *Scientific American*, October 1, 2014, https://www.scientificamerican.com /article/how-diversity-makes-us-smarter/.
4. Catalyst. Catalyst Quick Take: Turnover and Retention. New York: Catalyst, 2012.
5. Diane Downey, Tom March, and Adena Berkman, *Assimilating New Leaders: The Key to Executive Retention* (New York: AMACOM, 2001), 55.
6. William Shepherd, "Best Practices in Onboarding" (lecture, Bowling Green State University, Bowling Green, OH, November 18, 2014).
7. Talya N. Bauer, *Onboarding New Employees: Maximizing Success* (Alexandria, VA: SHRM Foundation, 2010), 1-2.
8. Bauer, *Onboarding New Employees*, 4-6.
9. Downey et al., *Assimilating New Leaders*, 56.

Chapter II

1. Frank Birkel, Steven R. Blackman, Jeff M. Hauswirth, Stephen G. Patscot, and Deborah Warburton, *Executive Onboarding: Is There a Right Way?* (Chicago, IL: Spencer Stuart, 2015), 3.

2. "20 Inspiring Quotes from Lao Tzu," *Habits for Wellbeing*, accessed January 5, 2017, http://www.habitsforwellbeing.com/20-inspiring-quotes-from-lao-tzu/.
3. Mark E. Van Buren and Todd Safferstone, "The Quick Wins Paradox," *Harvard Business Review*, January 2009, 57-59.
4. Marshall Goldsmith and Mark Reiter, *What Got You Here Won't Get You There: How Successful People Become Even More Successful* (New York: Hyperion, 2007), 99.
5. William Bridges, *Managing Transitions: Making the Most of Change*, 2nd ed. (Cambridge, MA: De Capo Press, 2003), 130.
6. Michael Watkins, *The First 90 Days: Critical Success Strategies for New Leaders at All Levels* (Boston, MA: Harvard Business School Press, 2003), 42.
7. Diane Downey, Tom March, and Adena Berkman, *Assimilating New Leaders: The Key to Executive Retention* (New York: AMACOM, 2001), 142.
8. Downey et al., *Assimilating New Leaders*, 143.
9. Lowell L. Bryan, Eric Matson, and Leigh M. Weiss, "Harnessing the Power of Informal Employee Networks," *McKinsey Quarterly*, November 2007, http://www.mckinsey.com/business-functions/organization/our-insights/harnessing-the-power-of-informal-employee-networks.
10. Goldsmith and Reiter, *What Got You Here*, 81-83.
11. Goldsmith and Reiter, *What Got You Here*, 17.

Chapter III

1. Avery Augustine, "3 Things Your Boss Is Worried About during Your First Week," *The Muse*, accessed May 1, 2016, https://www.themuse.com/advice/3-things-your-boss-is-worried-about-during-your-first-week.
2. David G. Allen, *Retaining Talent: A Guide to Analyzing and Managing Employee Turnover* (Alexandria, VA: SHRM Foundation, 2008), v.
3. *Oxford Living Dictionaries Online*, s.v. "risk management," accessed July 19, 2016, https://en.oxforddictionaries.com/.
4. Stephanie Henderson, "Onboarding—A Risk-Management Approach," *HR Strategy and Planning Excellence Essentials*, June 2014, 21-22.
5. David L. Dotlich, James L. Noel, and Norman Walker, *Leadership Passages: The Personal and Professional Transitions That Make or Break a Leader* (San Francisco, CA: Jossey-Bass, 2004), 35.
6. Ram Charan, Stephen Drotter, and James Noel, *The Leadership Pipeline: How to Build the Leadership-Powered Company* (San Francisco, CA: Jossey-Bass, 2001), 81.

7. John P. Wanous, "Installing a Realistic Job Preview: Ten Tough Choices," *Personnel Psychology* 42, no. 1 (1989): 117, doi:10.1111/j.1744 -6570.1989.tb01553.x.

8. Bill Barnett, "Understand a New Job (Before You Accept It)," *Harvard Business Review*, March 15, 2012, https://hbr.org/2012/03 /understand-a-new-job-before-you-accept-it.

Chapter IV

1. Cognisco, *$37 billion: Counting the Cost of Employee Misunderstanding* (Cranfield, UK: Cognisco Ltd., 2010).

2. Richard Davis and Linda Reese, "So You've Been Hired to Be a Chang Agent," accessed January 5, 2017, http://leaderonboarding .com/wp-content/uploads/2017/01/Hired-to-be-a-change-agent-20 16.pdf.

3. Ram Charan, Stephen Drotter, and James Noel, *The Leadership Pipeline: How to Build the Leadership-Powered Company*, 2nd ed. (San Francisco, CA: Jossey-Bass, 2011), xiv.

4. Diane Downey, Tom March, and Adena Berkman, *Assimilating New Leaders: The Key to Executive Retention* (New York: AMACOM, 2001), 136.

5. Marshall Goldsmith and Mark Reiter, *What Got You Here Won't Get You There: How Successful People Become Even More Successful* (New York: Hyperion, 2007), 100.

6. David L. Dotlich, James L. Noel, and Norman Walker, *Leadership Passages: The Personal and Professional Transitions That Make or Break a Leader* (San Francisco, CA: Jossey-Bass, 2004), 64.

7. Mary K. Suszko and James A. Breaugh, "The Effects of Realistic Job Previews on Applicant Self-Selection and Employee Turnover, Satisfaction, and Coping Ability," *Journal of Management* 12, no. 4 (1986): 513-23.

8. Bill Barnett, "Understand a New Job (Before You Accept It)," *Harvard Business Review*, March 15, 2015, https://hbr.org/2012/03 /understand-a-new-job-before-you-accept-it.

Chapter V

1. Nathan Bennett and G. James Lemoine, "What VUCA Really Means for You," *Harvard Business Review*, January/February 2014, https:// hbr.org/2014/01/what-vuca-really-means-for-you.

2. Ram Charan, Stephen Drotter, and James Noel, *The Leadership Pipeline: How to Build the Leadership-Powered Company* (San Francisco, CA: Jossey-Bass, 2001), 1.

3. Thomas J. DeLong and Vineeta Vijayaraghavan, "Let's Hear It for B Players," *Harvard Business Review*, June 2003, https://hbr.org/2003/06/lets-hear-it-for-b-players.

4. Robert K. Greenleaf, *Servant Leadership: A Journey into the Nature of Legitimate Power and Greatness*, 25th anniversary ed. (Mahwah, NJ: Paulist Press, 2002), 7.

5. Maura C. Ciccarelli, "Data vs. Discretion in Hiring," *Human Resources Executive Online*, December 17, 2015, http://www.hreonline.com/HRE/view/story.jhtml?id=534359659.

6. Joseph L. Bower, "The Most Successful CEOs Come from Within," *Harvard Business Review*, September 30, 2011, https://hbr.org/2011/09/most-successful-ceos.html.

7. Matthew Bidwell, "Paying More to Get Less: The Effects of External Hiring Versus Internal Mobility," *Administrative Science Quarterly* 56, no. 3 (September 2011): 369-407.

8. Michael I. Norton, Jeana H. Frost, and Dan Ariely, "Less Is More: The Lure of Ambiguity, or Why Familiarity Breeds Contempt," *Journal of Personality and Social Psychology* 92, no. 1 (January 2007): 97-105.

9. Corporate Leadership Council, *New Executive Assimilation Programs* (Arlington, VA: Corporate Executive Board, 2001), 3.

10. Eric Krell, "Weighing Internal Vs. External Hires," *HR Magazine*, January 7, 2015, https://www.shrm.org/hr-today/news/hr-magazine/pages/010215-hiring.aspx.

11. Amy Gallo, "How to Conduct an Internal Interview," *Harvard Business Review*, July 13, 2010, https://hbr.org/2010/07/how-to-conduct-an-internal-int.

12. See note 11 above.

13. Paul Spiegelman, "Don't Promote from Within: 5 Reasons," *Inc.*, March 28, 2012, http://www.inc.com/paul-spiegelman/why-you-should-not-promote-from-within.html.

14. David Wilkins, Alice Snell, and Bradford Thomas, "Emerging Leaders: Build Versus Buy—A White Paper by Taleo Research and Development Dimensions International," accessed July 30, 2016, http://www.ddiworld.com/ddi/media/white-papers/taleo-research-emerging-leaders-build-verse-buy_wp_taleo-ddi.pdf.

Chapter VI

1. Edgar H. Schein, *Organizational Culture and Leadership*, 3rd ed. (San Francisco, CA: Jossey-Bass, 2004), 23.

2. Diane Downey, Tom March, and Adena Berkman, *Assimilating New Leaders: The Key to Executive Retention* (New York: AMACOM, 2001), 223-25.

3. Daniel Denison, Robert Hooijberg, Nancy Lane, and Colleen Lief, *Leading Culture Change in Global Organizations: Aligning Culture and Strategy* (San Francisco, CA: Jossey-Bass, 2012), 3.

4. Michael Watkins, *The First 90 Days: Critical Success Strategies for New Leaders at All Levels* (Boston, MA: Harvard Business School Press, 2003), 53.

5. Edgar H. Schein, *Organizational Culture and Leadership: A Dynamic View* (San Francisco, CA: Jossey-Bass, 1985), 24.

6. Denison et al., *Leading Culture Change*, 6-18.

7. Denison et al., *Leading Culture Change*, 7.

8. David L. Dotlich, James L. Noel, and Norman Walker, *Leadership Passages: The Personal and Professional Transitions That Make or Break a Leader* (San Francisco, CA: Jossey-Bass, 2004), 36.

9. Downey et al., *Assimilating New Leaders*, 69.

10. Peter Barron Stark, "10 Traits of Leaders Who Successfully Drive Change," *Peter Barron Stark Companies* (blog), September 15, 2015, https://www.peterstark.com/traits-of-leaders-who-successfully-drive -change/.

11. John P. Kotter and James L. Heskett, *Corporate Culture and Performance* (New York: Free Press, 1992), 11.

Chapter VII

1. James. M. Kouzes and Barry Z. Posner, *Credibility: How Leaders Gain and Lose It, Why People Demand It*, 2nd ed. (San Francisco, CA: Jossey-Bass, 2011), xi.

2. Louis Quast, "Prevent Top Leader Derailment," *Talent Management* 8, no. 10 (2012): 42-43.

3. Michael Watkins, *The First 90 Days: Critical Success Strategies for New Leaders at All Levels* (Boston, MA: Harvard Business School Press, 2003), 36.

4. Mark E. Van Buren and Todd Safferstone, "The Quick Wins Paradox," *Harvard Business Review*, January 2009, 56.

5. Van Buren and Safferstone, "The Quick Wins Paradox," 59.

6. Ram Charan, Stephen Drotter, and James Noel, *The Leadership Pipeline: How to Build the Leadership-Powered Company*, 2nd ed. (San Francisco, CA: Jossey-Bass, 2011), 68.

Chapter VIII

1. Mark E. Van Buren and Todd Safferstone, "The Quick Wins Paradox," *Harvard Business Review*, January 2009, 55.

2. Frank Birkel, Steven R. Blackman, Jeff M. Hauswirth, Stephen G. Patscot, and Deborah Warburton, "Executive Onboarding: Is There

a Right Way," *Point of View* (blog), January 28, 2015, https://www.spencerstuart.com/research-and-insight/executive-onboarding.

3. Cynthia D. Fisher, "Social Support and Adjustment to Work: A Longitudinal Study," *Journal of Management* 11, no. 3 (1985): 39-53.

4. Susan Cocker, Anders Rasmussen, and Kevin Zander, "The CFO's First Hundred Days: A McKinsey Global Survey," *The McKinsey Quarterly*, December 2007, 8.

5. Marshall Goldsmith and Mark Reiter, *What Got You Here Won't Get You There: How Successful People Become Even More Successful*, (New York: Hyperion, 2007), 148.

6. Ram Charan, Stephen Drotter, and James Noel, *The Leadership Pipeline: How to Build the Leadership-Powered Company*, 2nd ed. (San Francisco, CA: Jossey-Bass, 2011), 44.

7. Charan et al., *The Leadership Pipeline*, 45.

Chapter IX

1. Tanya Menon and Leigh Thompson, "Envy at Work," *Harvard Business Review*, April 2010, 74.

2. Lisa Quast, "8 Tips to Transition from Co-Worker to Manager," *Forbes*, September 30, 2013, http://www.forbes.com/sites/lisaquast/2013/09/30/8-tips-to-transition-from-co-worker-to-manager/#77c31036575f.

3. David L. Dotlich, James L. Noel, and Norman Walker, *Leadership Passages: The Personal and Professional Transitions That Make or Break a Leader* (San Francisco, CA: Jossey-Bass, 2004), 98.

4. Marshall Goldsmith and Mark Reiter, *What Got You Here Won't Get You There: How Successful People Become Even More Successful* (New York: Hyperion, 2007), 68.

5. Doris Kearns Goodwin, *Team of Rivals: The Political Genius of Abraham Lincoln* (New York: Simon & Schuster, 2005), xvi.

Chapter X

1. Talya N. Bauer, *Onboarding New Employees: Maximizing Success* (Alexandria, VA: SHRM Foundation, 2010), 1.

2. Donna Hicks, *Dignity: Its Essential Role in Resolving Conflict*, rev. ed. (New Haven, CT: Yale University Press, 2013), 1.

3. Amy Gallo, "How to Get Feedback When You're the Boss," *Harvard Business Review*, May 15, 2012, https://hbr.org/2012/05/how-to-get-feedback-when-youre.

Chapter XI

1. Kevin P. Coyne and Edward J. Coyne Sr., "Surviving Your New CEO," *Harvard Business Review*, May 2007, 2.
2. Diane Downey, Tom March, and Adena Berkman, *Assimilating New Leaders: The Key to Executive Retention* (New York: AMACOM, 2001), 140-42.
3. David G. Allen, *Retaining Talent: A Guide to Analyzing and Managing Employee Turnover* (Alexandria, VA: SHRM Foundation, 2008), 3.
4. Roger Schwarz, "Taking Over from an Incompetent Team Leader," *Harvard Business Review*, November 18, 2013, https://hbr.org/2013/11/taking-over-from-an-incompetent-team-leader.
5. Downey et al., *Assimilating New Leaders*, 136-37.

Chapter XII

1. Marshall Goldsmith and Mark Reiter, *What Got You Here Won't Get You There: How Successful People Become Even More Successful* (New York: Hyperion, 2007), 42.

Chapter XIII

1. "Managing Employee Relocation," Society for Human Resource Management, last modified November 22, 2015, https://www.shrm.org/resourcesandtools/tools-and-samples/toolkits/pages/managingemployeerelocation.aspx.
2. Suzanne Lucas, "How to Get a Job As a 'Trailing Spouse,'" *Money Watch*, February 26, 2014, http://www.cbsnews.com/news/how-to-get-a-job-as-a-trailing-spouse/.
3. Diane Schmidt, "10 Ways to Help Your Teens Deal with Moving to a New Home," *About Home*, April 14, 2016, http://moving.about.com/od/movingwithchildre1/a/help_teens_move.htm.
4. Ellen J. Wallach, "How to Relocate Happily When You're Single," *The Wall Street Journal*, August 17, 1999, http://on.wsj.com/14wht9J.
5. Illustration used with permission. Diane Downey, Tom March, and Adena Berkman, *Assimilating New Leaders: The Key to Executive Retention* (New York: AMACOM, 2001), 35.
6. Brian Tracy, "4 Ways to Maintain a Positive Attitude and Keep Moving Forward, Even When You're Stressed," *Brian Tracy International* (blog), accessed August 31, 2016, http://www.briantracy.com/blog/personal-success/how-to-manage-stress-and-overcome-difficulties-4-ways-to-maintain-a-positive-attitude-and-keep-moving-forward/.

7. Diane Schmidt, "How to Meet New People in Your Neighborhood after Moving," *About Home*, August 12, 2016, http://moving.about.com/od/settlingintips/qt/make_friends.htm.

8. South Carolina Department of Mental Health Office of Client Affairs, *Making a Difference: How to Become and Remain Active in Your Community—A Guide to Volunteering*, accessed September 7, 2016, http://www.state.sc.us/dmh/client_affairs/volunteer_guide.pdf.

Chapter XIV

1. Mark A. Stein and Lilith Christiansen, *Successful Onboarding: Strategies to Unlock Hidden Value Within Your Organization* (New York: McGraw-Hill Education, 2010), 3.

Index

Acknowledgements

Thank you to our clients and colleagues who were catalysts for the creation of structured, innovative, and sustainable onboarding methodologies and tools. We appreciate your open-mindedness and willingness to both acknowledge and address the challenges inherent as leaders transition to new roles.

Early influencers and thought partners included Diane Downey, Edward Ferris, Ron Cadieux, Dan Denison, Brett Avner, Bill Butler, Mike Holland, and Sue Edwards. We value those who expanded their understanding of onboarding to pioneer approaches that benefited many leaders and organizations, including Tim Reynolds, Mark Markram, Barb Daly, Kreg Gruber, Robin Fisher-Welch, Kim Geyer, Linda Slawinski, Christian Gianni, Lisa Morris, Mauro Piloni, Russ Brock, and Justin Taylor. More recent partners include Hugh Sherman, Tammy Patrick, Tom Jessep, Maarten Putz, Maureen Metcalf, Sri Ramkumar, Samantha Maxwell-Reed, and Michelle Reese.

Our colleagues at *Leader OnBoarding* have made the growth and success of our work possible: Sandee Workman, Joy M. Hall, Alex Evdokimenko, and Cindy Bartholomew; and coaches who have partnered with us: Andrea Thomas, Susan Alexander, Dave Gettles, and Greg Bliss.

Linda Reese sends a special thank you to her mother, Emily Jean McFadden, for her inspiring influence as a personal and professional role model.

And finally, we wish to acknowledge our intellectual forbearer Diane Downey whose unique approach to leader transition inspired and informed our work; and her colleague Amy Kates, who shares our passion for ensuring Diane's enduring legacy.

64104789R00122

Made in the USA
Lexington, KY
28 May 2017